T0208578

# ILLUSION AND REALITY

# ILLUSION AND REALITY

## The Meaning of Anxiety

*David Smail*

Routledge
Taylor & Francis Group

LONDON AND NEW YORK

First published 1984 by J.M. Dent & Sons Ltd
Revised edition published in 1997 by Constable and Company Ltd

This edition published in 2015 by
Karnac Books Ltd

Published 2018 by Routledge
2 Park Square, Milton Park, Abingdon, Oxon OX14 4RN
711 Third Avenue, New York, NY 10017, USA

*Routledge is an imprint of the Taylor & Francis Group,
an informa business*

**British Library Cataloguing in Publication Data**
A C.I.P. for this book is available from the British Library

ISBN: 9781782202851 (pbk)

# Contents

# Preface to Constable edition

*Illusion and Reality* is the first of a series of (so far) four books which attempt to place the experience of psychological distress within the social environment which gives rise to it. The other three are *Taking Care, The Origins of Unhappiness* and *How to Survive Without Psychotherapy*. With hindsight (and in reassuring confirmation of the psychological theory they elaborate!) it is possible to see how each of these books is shaped by the context in which it was written.

Being the first, *Illusion and Reality* examines the predicament of the individual person from the perspective of the person him/herself (the later works travel progressively further out into the social environment in order to pinpoint the origins of distress). Above all else it is about the individual's subjective view of the world and the injuries done to his or her subjectivity by the world into which (as the existentialists would say) s/he is thrown.

Being conceived and written in the early nineteen-eighties, it is also, I now see, about the predicament of people (i.e. all of us) who were caught up in the disintegration of 'old' certainties (the 'post-war consensus') which were in any case largely illusory (hence, in part, the title) and at the mercy of brutal market forces which were about to sweep them up and toss them into a torrent of change and insecurity. Although I would change very little in my analysis of subjectivity, I think perhaps I do accord it a little too much independent power. What the later nineteen-eighties and the nineties have made starkly apparent is just how vulnerable we are to social forces operating far beyond our personal spheres of influence, and though some of the more obvious threats seem to have changed (the nuclear threat, for example, seems to have receded) the subjective person is if anything even more embattled against apparently irresistible, largely economic, pressures than was the case fifteen years ago.

But if our subjective voice is weaker, it is all the more important that we should be able to recognize its cry, and the kinds of pointers to the significance of subjective experience and its expression, the clinical examples of which I made use, are I think as relevant now as they were then.

Anxiety is a sign, an indication of a sometimes terrifying disillusionment in which safe myths about the conditions of our existence become peeled away to reveal an altogether less reassuring form of knowledge about the world. The point of this book, though its outlook may at times seem rather bleak, is, however, precisely one of reassurance: that the unnerving knowledge we may possess of a hard and painful reality represents in fact a true insight into the way things are and not a form of craziness.

If anything, illusory ideals of living envelop our subjectivity even more oppressively than they did at the time this book was written. The triumphant progress of 'marketing' – the colossal investment of intelligence, ingenuity and technical sophistication which perfects the arts by which we are seduced into consumerist culture – has put significant sections of a whole generation out of touch with the social and biological bases of reality. I have accordingly been struck in very recent times by the number of young people I encounter (people for whom the late seventies to the mid-nineties constituted the formative years of their lives) who have not just, so to speak, fallen for the advertising, but have invested their lives, energies, ambitions – have indeed *put their faith* – in a glossy, fashionable world of apparent social ease and affluence which they have helped to create and come to inhabit, but in which they are at the same time assailed by a profound insecurity about who they are and how they figure in relation to others.

These are not people who function poorly or, as the psychiatrists like to say, 'inadequately', in the modern world – indeed they are often socially, educationally and vocationally very successful – but they suffer from what is to me a new form of anxiety (new, anyway, in its pervasiveness). Deeply troubling though not disabling, the discomfort and unhappiness of their actual experience of themselves contrasts strangely with the apparently ideal existence they have managed to achieve. Fulfilled ambition and a kind of biological unease exist side-by-side; realized ideals bring no gratification but only a sense of being cut loose from embodied reality – far from being buoyed up by success the body may even seem to collapse under an invisible strain, giving rise, for example, to pains in the back or the bowels.

These are, so it seems, young people who have received too little instruction in what it is to be human, how to recognize and take account of what their own bodies tell them about their relations with the world. As a result, they are not able to interpret the promptings of their own subjectivity. For them, 'reality' has become the production of a 'postmodern' apparatus of media-generated images with which no embodied relatedness is possible. But the body, even if rendered irrelevant to the fashionable universe of discourse, still has to be lived in.

Central to this 'new' form of anxiety is the sense that achievement is empty of satisfaction – what the person is *supposed* to want, and so acquires, he or she simply does not desire. A life conditioned by marketed ideals of 'success' can become so detached from subjective bodily desire that the person simply finds it impossible to say what he or she wants, and 'pleasing oneself', even (or rather especially) in such basic wants as food or sex, can become something which has to be assiduously learned from scratch. Such anxiety is reduced through coming to experience, refine and elaborate the *desire* which links body to world. As always, however, the cost of becoming free from marketed illusions is the possibility of exposure to real pain, i.e. pain which is instantly identifiable as stemming from the injuries inflicted on embodied individuals by a far from perfect social environment. In other words, 'disillusionment' is a precondition for true experience.

The 'official' institutions through which people may seek to understand the experience of anxiety have, sadly, gained in neither sophistication nor validity since this book was first published in 1984. Psychiatry has if anything retrenched to its traditional position of biological explanation and physical treatment, with a touch of social Darwinism thrown in. No doubt such retrenchment is in response at least partly to financial starvation and pressures to contain the politically defined 'seriously mentally ill' who might otherwise become too conspicuous a blot on the landscape created by 'care in the community'. The deregulation of the market in health care has let loose a flood of 'alternative' approaches to therapy and counselling which are remarkable only for the illusoriness of their promises and the childlike wishfulness of their 'theories'. With counsellors on hand, apparently, to soothe away the ravages of reality in almost any eventuality, the authentic voice of the subjective person has become muffled to the point of extinction.

There is a tragic irony in the fact that the vast majority of people who come to consult clinical psychologists like me tend to be those who find it most difficult to abandon their personal conviction in the truth of their subjective experience. Not that this is an intellectual process that they themselves would recognize; it is an emotional one. The inability to abandon a fundamentally true insight into the nature of the social world in favour of a convenient illusion is reflected in psychological pain – though 'psychological' here is too abstract and insubstantial a word for something which is so firmly embodied. Emotional distress, far from being an indication that something is wrong with the person, is far more likely to point to something wrong with his/her world. As much as anything, this book is about the possibility of understanding the 'language' of pain.

Perhaps all distinguishable eras of social development are characterized by their regnant ideological illusions. It sometimes seems to me that maybe 'psychology' is one of the principal illusions of the twentieth century. The raw materials of emotional distress are much more bodies and worlds than they are psychologies. Distress arises from the subjection of the embodied person to social forces over which s/he has very little control. 'Psychology', such as it is, arises out of the person's struggle to understand and conceptualize the nature of his/her experience. It is a matter of meaning. But changing the experience of distress cannot, either logically or practically, be achieved purely by trying to operate on the meanings to which the body-world interaction gives rise. Yet this is precisely the mistake psychology, in particular of course therapeutic psychology, has made. It is as if we can eradicate the experience of distress by changing the way we think or talk about it. Pure magic.

This book spells out the beginnings of an alternative understanding. Even so it is undoubtedly not without its own illusions. One that I can discern quite easily after the passage of thirteen years is my misplaced deference to Freudian theory and my too sweeping condemnation of behaviourism. Psychoanalysis (as Richard Webster's comprehensive refutation of Freud demonstrates*) derailed us right at the beginning of the century from developing with anything approaching scientific validity a view of the way people suffer emotional distress not because of who they are but because of what is done to them. Behaviourism – in, admittedly, a hopelessly inadequate and ludicrously over-simplified manner – at least made some kind of effort to put us back on the rails. In any event, the only possible ground upon which our illusions can be stripped away, upon which we can start the essential process of disillusionment, is that of our subjective experience. For it is here and only here that reality reveals itself to us.

David Smail
Nottingham, March 1997

* Richard Webster, *Why Freud Was Wrong*, HarperCollins, 1995.

# 1   The Myth of Normality

This book is written in the hope that it may help remove some of the mystery which surrounds psychological distress, not just from an abstract point of view, but in terms which make concrete sense to people who are frightened or anxious about aspects of their lives which they experience as abnormal. My choice of the terms 'abstract' and 'concrete', rather than 'theoretical' and 'practical', is deliberate, because it seems to me that it is precisely through a *theoretical* framework that the nature of psychological distress can best be confronted, and to some extent alleviated. For reasons which I shall discuss in a later chapter, it seems to me that an adequate theory – i.e., an explicit set of ideas or concepts – is exactly what most people have no access to when trying to get to grips with 'symptoms' of their psychological malaise, and this is why such 'symptoms' seem, often, so mysterious: while one may concede that there are 'experts' who *do* understand them, one cannot, it seems, understand them oneself, and, without recourse to these experts, cannot expect to.

I have been careful not to raise my sights higher than expressing a hope that this book may contribute to a 'demystification' of psychological distress, and that is because I certainly do not believe that it could 'cure' such distress in individual readers. Although the popular culture, as well as many 'experts', makes an equation between psychological 'symptoms' and illness, with the implication that individuals play host to such symptoms in the way they might to symptoms of, say, appendicitis (with similar possibilities for 'cure') it seems clear to me that human misery, of which psychological distress forms a significant part, does not crop up, as it were, *within* individual people, but arises out of the interaction of people with each other and from the nature of the world we have created. Until we change the way we act towards each other, and the social institutions we have constructed, we shall not get much relief from the symptoms of anxiety, depression and despair which beset all of us at some times in our lives, and some of us nearly all the time. The 'experts' will not change the world – they will simply make a satisfactory living helping people to adjust to it; the world will only change when ordinary people realize what is making them unhappy, and do something about it. To arrive at such a realization, they will first, I believe, have to develop a proper conceptual grasp of the roots of their distress.

'Changing the world' is, of course, largely a political enterprise, and political issues are by no means irrelevant to psychological and psychiatric disorder. This is not, however, to be a sweeping political tract: people experience misery and despair within the immediate context of their own lives and relationships, and it is within this arena that they have to get to grips with them. I wish to suggest not so much that people must change the world (though that would be nice!) as that they must change *their* worlds, and that to do that they must first develop their *own* grasp of what is happening in that limited, personal world in which they pursue their existence.

This is not, then, to be a 'self-help' book in the sense of 'what to do about your anxiety' or 'how to overcome your fears and be a more successful person', etc. There are many such books, and many of them, indeed, contain elements of fairly sound practical advice. They are nearly all, however, books whose aim is to *adjust* the reader to a world which is taken as *given*, as simply real and there and to be reckoned with, but not altered. This is, at least tacitly, to see 'symptoms' as arising *within* individuals in exactly the way that I believe to be false, and it is therefore an enterprise which must be doomed to failure in any fundamental respect.

In my work as a psychotherapist, I find many patients who have turned at one time or another to self-help books (of the kind that this is not) in the hope of finding some quick, relatively painless solution to their difficulties. Some patients, undoubtedly, have been significantly helped by such books, one or two to a quite profound extent, but on the whole most seem to find them curiously unsatisfying, however sensible the advice they contain appears to be. Partly, no doubt, this is because, to be effective, psychological help is best given in the context of a living human relationship. But also, I suspect, the relative lack of impact of such books lies in their failure to offer a theoretical account of the nature and origins of psychological distress which is both accurate *and* makes sense to 'ordinary' people.

Again, in my work with patients, I have found that it is through unravelling with them some of the *conceptual* mysteries surrounding their 'symptoms' – the ideas, that is, that they have about them – that enough progress is made for them to get down to tackling their difficulties and dilemmas in ways which make a practical difference to their lives. This, usually, is not to 'cure' their 'symptoms', but to bring them face-to-face with circumstances in their lives which are painful and distressing, and which they can ignore only at the cost of 'neurotic' suffering. Often, admittedly, this is to replace one kind of suffering with another, and whether or not this seems a good idea depends on one's values. To me, it seems more constructive, and essentially more hopeful, to recognize that real difficulties, real evils and real pain arise in the world around us through our conduct towards one another, than to resort, albeit unawares, to self-deceiving strategies which, for example, allow 'illness' to provide the explanation, and indeed the form, of our misery.

It is, then, in the hope that some of what I have learned through my work with people in distress may prove of use to others that this book is written. It will cure nobody's predicament, but I hope it may help some to confront theirs with greater understanding and courage than might otherwise have been the case.

It has never been my feeling that the 'patients' who have consulted me over the years are 'abnormal' in any particularly meaningful sense, though it is often the case that they have been defined as such by others (family, friends, doctors, psychiatrists and other professional colleagues) or by themselves. It seems likely to me that it is the extent rather than the kind of unhappiness which drives someone to seek professional help, and it seems therefore logical to conclude that there must be many, probably a majority of people who have not yet been driven that far but who are almost equally unhappy. The problems of 'patients', that is, point to a malaise which is likely to be general among 'normal' people in our society rather than specific to a particular, relatively small group of people who are thought to have succumbed to some kind of personal inadequacy.

There is in my view absolutely no convincing evidence that the kinds of difficulties complained of by the vast majority of people who consult psychiatrists, psychologists and psychotherapists are the result of any kind of 'illness', mental or otherwise, and yet this is the explanation most widely subscribed to in our society. If I am right – and I am certainly not alone in taking such a view – then what is needed is a more satisfactory account of how such difficulties arise, and one which is available to, as well as understandable by, 'ordinary' people, i.e. people other than the 'experts' whose job it is to develop an understanding of such matters. In fact, there are many such e*x*perts who have, I believe, developed accounts of psychological distress which are far more illuminating and useful than those current in our general culture, and from this point of view there is very little new in what I shall be saying. However, it does seem to me time that the experts stopped simply talking to each other and started trying to make their ideas and concepts available to those 'ordinary' people who are in the best position to make constructive use of them, or, failing that, at least deserve the chance to pass judgment on how useful such ideas and concepts might be.

Let me start my own attempt at this enterprise, then, with some observations which may seem fairly obvious, but which, I believe, on the whole we fail to take seriously. These observations centre round the tacit belief to which most of us subscribe that the majority of people are by and large pretty well adjusted, contented, and lead conventionally well ordered lives.

In contrast to this happy state of affairs – indeed, partly because of the belief that it is so – it seems to me that most people keep the way they feel about themselves as a deep and shameful secret. Much of our waking life is spent in a desperate struggle to persuade others that we are not what we fear ourselves to be, or what they may discover us to be if they see through our pretences. Most people, most of the time, have a profound and unhappy awareness of the contrast between what they *are* and what they *ought* to be. Even at a relatively superficial (but extremely pervasive) level, for example, many people feel weak and silly when they ought to be strong and confident, ugly and insignificant when they should be attractive and striking. As a consequence of this we spend enormous amounts of time and energy in guarding against others' getting a glimpse of our 'true', shameful selves by constructing what we feel will be acceptable public versions of ourselves, but which we know to be a hollow sham (unless, that is, we come after a while to believe in our own posturing, fall for our own 'image').

The aim that society sets us is to *be* something: to be recognized in at least some sphere, and if only by our immediate family and acquaintances, as successful or admirable or in some way to be reckoned with. What you *do* matters not half as much as the aggrandizement which doing it brings you. The very word 'successful' – perhaps most properly applied to actions – is now more usually applied to people; there are a few people who are happy if their activities are attended by success, but many more whose idea of happiness is to be *seen* as a 'successful person' no matter how dubious the route by which they achieve it.

Behind many 'symptoms' of anxiety lies an injury to the person's self-esteem, a despairing, inarticulate awareness that he or she has not lived up to the standards of adequacy which we are all complicit in setting. The most obvious ideal, of course, is that, as well as successful, you should be strong, confident, attractive and powerful; the world is your oyster, and if you fail to find a comfortable place in it, there must be something the matter with you.

However banal it may seem, nothing holds up to us the nature of our aspirations better than television advertisements. In the early days of the medium, perhaps it was possible to see television advertisements as little more than naive and transparent, but sometimes quite amusing, lies, but now, though we may think we take them with a pinch of salt, they confront us almost remorselessly with the ideals we cannot live up to: the happy, loving family eating their cornflakes against views of waving wheatfields, eagerly waiting for the joys of the day to unfold; slim, beautiful women whose smooth and un-blemished limbs slide effortlessly into blue denim skins, later to catch the strong and approving gaze of confident young men who will cherish them with just the right amount of lust; unwrinkled middle-aged couples, with lovely children, whose new washing machine unites them in a love burning only just less brightly than on their wedding night; mature, square-jawed men whose credit cards place the world of travel and technology instantly within their knowing grasp; beer-drinking workers who know how to be men in a man's world; wielders of power tools who cast contemptuous eyes over their neighbours' botched jobs; people who know the ropes and fit into the world, handle others with easy assurance, get what they want without ruffling any feathers, live their lives in material ease, basking in the admiration and affection of those around them, but being tough if they have to be.

Perhaps not everyone has quite lost sight of how far in fact the ideals to which television advertising gives a caricatured, but nevertheless accurate, outer form are really impossible of achievement in the world we actually live in, but there are very many people who are cast into despair because of their failure to live up to them. Although we should be successful, confident, in control, even-tempered, honest, honourable, likeable, bold, etc., etc., our actual experience of ourselves, as far as we can bear to look at it, is quite otherwise, and to get a really clear view of the motives and intentions of our actions is almost inevitably to be assailed with anxiety because we are so unlike what we are supposed to be.

At another level, the ideal world is represented as well as upheld by its institutions. As people, we succeed or fail to the extent to which we manage to live up to the standards set for us by the educational, political, legal, cultural and social establishment. It is from such institutions, and their representatives, that we gain our ideas about what is right, true, and real, as well as about what kinds of personal characteristics are admirable. We accord the representatives of our institutions with all the qualities we know ourselves to lack: the experts are expert, the educated clever and knowledgeable, politicians have our interests at heart, scientists are wise, doctors know how to cure disease, lawyers are motivated by a concern for justice. The rich, successful and aristocratic, the 'personalities' and household names, the celebrities and stars live lives somehow bigger and more significant than our own; their births, marriages and deaths are to be celebrated or mourned on a par with (sometimes even more than) those within our own families. These, it seems, are ideal people representing an ideal world, people whose outward characteristics we may strive to imitate even if we can never really hope to attain their status, people who have broken free of our own doubts and uncertainties, anxiety and shame. The secrets of power, wisdom and knowledge are available to only some members of our society, and are enshrined in institutions to which only things like a knighthood, a Ph.D. or 'stardom' gain access, though we may share in this kind of ultimate reality by identifying ourselves with its values. Most of us seem to have lost sight of the fact that our institutions are created by people like ourselves – are, indeed, our own creations – but instead experience them as unalterably, objectively real, part of the world which it would just not make sense to question. You might, it is true, see your teacher or your doctor as fallible, but you are less likely to challenge the standards represented by education or medicine as institutions: the *values* embedded in our institutions, that is, we tend to see as fixed, unquestionable and obviously correct.

Looking at the world around them, few people can escape getting a fairly clear impression of what it is to 'fit in' to our society, what it is to be normal, competent and stable. Even if we cannot all achieve the *ideals* of confidence, attractiveness, power and success, at least we can expect to be *normal*. For example, if you are a man, this might mean being able to perform your job satisfactorily and reasonably successfully, at the same time getting on all right with your fellow workers, providing at least adequately for your family, enjoying a satisfactory social life, being a good sexual partner, being able to stand up effectively to unfair opposition, and so on. If you are a woman, you may find that as well as having to fulfil some of the above expectations in relation to your job and should also be able to run a home properly, bear and bring up children rewardingly, look attractive, get on with your in-laws, enjoy the company of other mothers (especially if you are not working), be sexually responsive, and so on. The *norms* for how we should be are all around us, everywhere, all the time: we learn them from our parents and at school, see them apparently exemplified by our friends and neighbours, imbibe them from the television, have them, as I have said, enshrined in our institutions. Though fame and stardom and brilliant success may clearly not be achievable, anyone ought to be able to cope with the basic requirements presented by life.

If you *cannot* cope with these basic requirements, you are likely to conclude that there is something the matter with you – you are not *normal*. Unless you have a lot of courage and a strong belief in yourself, you are not likely to conclude that it is the norms themselves which are wrong. If you do conclude that you are not normal, you are likely to feel anxiety and shame, and you are likely to want to keep the extent of your abnormality a fairly closely guarded secret. It is of course likely that you are not the only one to be nursing a secret fear that you do not come up to the standards set by our society, but because other people too keep their shame to themselves, it becomes impossible to share the experience of 'inadequacy', and it looks as though just about everyone is normal except you.

In fact, it is my contention that the ideal world in which we profess belief is riddled with myth, and that the secret world of anxiety and pain in which we actually live our lives is the real one which we truly share. *Why* this should be so it is not my present aim to attempt to clarify, because this would take us beyond the individual's immediate experience; what I want to establish first is that the kind of experience we are so ready to call abnormal is in fact almost universal, for only in coming to gain an *accurate* grasp of our predicament will we be able to see beyond it to the possibility of changing it.

Any inquiry into the nature of and reasons for a person's psychological distress must progress through a number of levels of varying complexity. At the most superficial level is the statement of the 'problem'. Frequently, one can see quite clearly in this the contrast between how people feel and how they think they *ought* to feel; there is also often a contrast between how people appear (in fact as quite 'normal') and how they are afraid they appear (as 'abnormal' or even 'crazy'). In presenting the following brief examples of 'problems', all I want to do is suggest that the kinds of things that people who have come to me as patients complain of are not signs of 'abnormality' or 'illness', but are in many cases typical of feelings we all share to a greater or lesser extent at various times in our lives. They do, however, present us with a challenge to our understanding. I have chosen 'cases' of kinds which occur very frequently in most therapists' experience, and though I have kept them utterly realistic, I have for obvious reasons not described any individually recognizable person (though I hope many readers may be able to recognize *themselves* at least indirectly among these descriptions). Although, in some instances, a kind of explanation for the difficulties and feelings described may be to varying degrees apparent, it is not at this stage my intention to focus on explanation, but merely to establish the breadth and generality of manifestations of the experience of psychological pain.

*Frank is a handsome, friendly, well dressed man just turned forty. He was the bright boy in his family – the only one who went to grammar school. He went to university, and eventually became an accountant. He is ambitious and successful. But most mornings he awakens sick with dread at what the day might bring. At first he could not understand why he should feel so 'ill', but it now seems that at least part of the problem is that he's tortured by the fear that friends and colleagues, and even his wife, will 'realize' what a phoney he is, that all his qualifications and success have somehow, as he feels it, been achieved under false pretences. If people knew, for example, how hard he had had to work for his exams, they would realize that he is not very clever at all. His promotion at work only came about because of the sudden death of one of his competitors for the job, who was in fact (in his view) by far the most able. Every day, he feels, he is likely to make some fatally stupid error at work that will expose him for the fraud he really is. Now their children are a bit older, his wife is taking a course in business studies and may well end up doing a responsible job more competently than he, and then she too will see through his façade and lose interest in him. Quite often, he feels so umanned by this that his sexual performance is affected, which makes him feel all the more weak and inadequate.*

*Arthur is a turner in an engineering shop. He has always been shy and sensitive, and never had many friends. He was not much good at football at school, though that was all his father was interested in his being. He has one or two interests which his workmates find unusual — he likes antiques, and reads books on ancient history. The men at work talk most of the time about cars, sex and football, and cannot understand why Arthur has not got a girlfriend. He worries about being thought homosexual, and sometimes suspects that people are talking about him behind his back. He feels awkward and stupid and blushes a great deal. He longs in secret for a girlfriend, but feels that, unlike his workmates, he has not got the dash and know-how to get one, and if a girl does show any interest in him he shies away in the fear that she would expose him as sexually incompetent. At twenty-five, he still lives at his parents' home, spending most of his time in his room listening to records and reading. He is a pleasant, good-looking, quietly spoken young man, and none of those around him realize how painful he finds his life.*

*At eighteen, Susan went to live with a man only a few years older. She had known him for a couple of years, and was attracted by his exuberance and apparent mastery of life; she liked his sense of humour, and nothing seemed to get him down. She loved him, as she put it, wholeheartedly, and devoted herself to his needs. She got pregnant, but though she wanted the baby, had an abortion because her boyfriend said he would leave her if she did not. A year later he left her to pursue an affair with a married woman. Although they had had a lot of rows, and he had hit her on several occasions, once actually breaking one of her fingers, she missed him desperately and could not imagine making a relationship with anyone else. Though she does not look it, Susan is obsessed with the feeling that she is too fat. She tries to starve herself, but spoils it all by going on sudden binges of eating cream cakes, and then has to make herself sick to get rid of them. She feels that she is in some way revolting, and deserves nobody's love.*

*Joan is at a loss to understand why she cannot go shopping on her own without becoming so dizzy, sick and breathless that she is afraid of fainting, even dying, on the street. At first she thought she must have some unusual, and possibly even fatal, illness but now she realizes that the feeling which overcomes her is of fear – intense, crippling panic. But she can think of no reason for her fear – there seems to be nothing in her life so out of the ordinary that it could account for such extreme feelings. She has two healthy little children, a hard-working husband who has already made enough for them to buy their own house, and her mother, who was always a great support, lives not far away. She was very ashamed of her 'symptoms' at first, and went to great lengths to disguise them – she would make excuses not to have to go out on her own, or would try to arrange it so that her husband, or a neighbour with whom she was on fairly friendly terms, would come with her. But finally it began to haunt her so much that, secretly, she had to go and confess it all to her doctor.*

*Mary lives in what is by most standards a very large house in a very smart suburb, and is married to a very well-off, successful and good-looking businessman. She has two daughters who go to private boarding schools, a car of her own, and plenty of help with the house. And yet she wakes up every morning long before it is time to get up, feeling an overwhelming sense of unease and a kind of hopeless, dead futility. Her day is a nightmare of unreality and pointlessness. She stands in her beautifully equipped kitchen trying to plan the menu for a dinner party, but stares out of the window at a garden from which, though the sun is shining brightly, all the colour seems to have been drained. With tears rolling down her face, she goes back to bed and lies staring at the ceiling. For seven years she has been receiving treatment for her 'depression', is on permanent medication and has had electric shock treatment, but all more or less to no avail. To her friends and acquaintances, however, she seems poised and assured, intelligent and charming.*

*The Masons seem to their friends, families, colleagues and neighbours a particularly happy and united family. Husband and wife both have quite responsible and rewarding jobs, and their two children are outgoing and friendly, and successful at school. And yet, for ten years, Mrs Mason has been in love with another man, though their affair had been very short-lived. Her children and their father had been very close, and she had wished to give them, and him, no pain, so she stayed with them, and her lover eventually married someone else and went to live in another part of the country. But she spends her life with a constant awareness of loneliness, of missing something of which, in any case, she got only a very brief glimpse. She suspects that her husband also feels lonely, but probably without knowing why.*

*Apart from feeling despairing, broken and angry, what Mrs Robertson finds most difficult is trying to make sense of how, completely out of the blue, her husband could leave her and their three teenage children to go off with a woman fifteen years younger than himself. She sees no future for herself and thinks a lot about suicide, but knows that the children need her. Her two sons took their father's departure fairly well, but her daughter has become difficult to handle.*

*About eighteen months after the birth of her second baby, Sheila started to develop a kind of panicky fear that she might accidentally be endangering her own and other people's children. She spent a lot of time checking that she had not left knives where they could be reached, that she had not somehow injured the baby when bathing him, that she had not dropped something into prams which she passed in the street, possibly smothering their occupants. After a while the checking began to dominate her life, though she concealed it quite skilfully. It also extended to other things – she might have left windows open, doors unlocked, the telephone off the hook.*

*Brian, a fairly senior civil servant whose job requires him to travel quite frequently between large British cities, suddenly developed an embarrassing fear of trains – particularly those which have to travel through tunnels of some length, and his worst fear was of getting trapped on a train which had come to a halt in a tunnel. At first he would sit through the ordeal of train journeys with his jaw clenched, white and damp with dread, but then it got too much and he had to start making excuses about not being able for one reason or another to make the journeys his job demanded. Eventually that would no longer wash, and so, shamefaced, he went to his doctor.*

*Walter was so good at football at school that he was given a trial for a first division club, which was enthusiastic about his prospects. But, in his late teens, he found reasons for giving up his sporting ambitions and became an apprentice joiner instead. The trouble was that Walter felt (unreasonably, according to those who have examined him medically) that his penis was*

*unusually small, and the ordeal of communal changing rooms
became impossible for him to bear, even though nobody had ever
said anything.*

*For as long as she can remember, Brenda bore the brunt of
her father's rage. Sometimes when sober, and nearly always
when drunk, he would shout at her and hit her without provoca-
tion. Her mother got much the same treatment, but dealt with
the whole situation by keeping out of the way as much as
possible and meekly doing her husband's bidding. So when, at
the age of sixteen, Brenda met Tom, it was for her like a gift
from heaven — he was so kind and understanding, relaxed and
easy-going. So she ran off with him when she was seventeen and
married him when she was eighteen. Their friends think they
make a lovely couple, but Brenda is in despair because she has
lost all her sexual feelings: she cannot bear Tom to touch her,
though a nicer, kinder, more tolerant husband she could not
wish to have.*

People who have experienced 'symptoms' of the kinds described above often characterize them as having occurred out of
the blue, and have no idea about what, if anything, may have
made them vulnerable to them. As this book progresses I shall
consider why it is that states such as these seem, often, so
mysterious and unpredictable, but the point to bear in mind for
the moment is that, whether or not these people had any
understanding of what led up to their condition, all of them felt
out of step in some way with those around them, whose lives
seemed almost tauntingly normal, stable and happy in comparison with the pain, shame and often secret despair they themselves felt. They seemed to themselves, in other words, outside
the norms of our society. It rarely occurred to any of them that,
to others, they appeared perfectly normal themselves – if anything it would have seemed to them that, in some form or other,
their differentness from other people would be observable at a
glance.

Not only did most of these people feel abnormal, misfits in an
otherwise smoothly functioning world, but many experienced
themselves as having 'broken down' – or at least as 'having a
breakdown' or being in danger of having one. Again, I shall
discuss in a later chapter the kinds of explanation for 'breakdowns' which our society offers, but, until they had become
drawn into the 'official' apparatus which exists for helping
those in distress of the kinds mentioned above, these people

were by and large bereft of any plausible explanation for their misery apart from a feeling that they were in some way inadequate or at fault. It did not, for example, occur to them that their experience was the *natural* outcome of a particular state of affairs – the reasonable upshot of their life history, so to speak – nor on the whole were they encouraged in such a belief when they were eventually driven to consult the experts. Still less did it occur to them that their state might be one commonly experienced by others: that is, not only natural, but frequent. For a variety of reasons, people are extremely reticent about revealing their worries and vulnerabilities to others, which, as I have already suggested, reinforces a view of the social world, subscribed to wittingly or unwittingly by most of us, which is in fact much more a myth than an accurate picture of reality. Even more seriously, people are not simply careful to keep quiet about their private fears – they are often unable even to see for themselves what they are. It is as if we have no proper system of ideas nor a proper language with which to understand and describe our feelings, but must rely on 'symptoms' to give them some kind of communicable form.

I do not believe that there can be anybody who has reached beyond the tenderest years without experiencing acute psychological pain over his or her feelings of inadequacy in relation to others, anxiety about his or her performance of socially expected functions and tasks, depression or despair at some kind of failure or loss. There can be very few people who have not at some time experienced so-called 'symptoms' of anxiety, whether it be exaggerated fears about their appearance (their physical adequacy), lapses in sexual performance, fears of insects or animals, or heights, of meeting others or being made in some way conspicuous in groups of people, of being exposed to ridicule by the opposite sex (or by their own sex – there are many men who find it impossible to urinate in even the threatened presence of others in public lavatories, many women for whom communal fitting rooms in clothes shops are a torture).

There are, however, quite a lot of people who *claim* to live lives unruffled by such shames and embarrassments, who make a show of adequacy which is to the envy of their friends and to the chagrin of those who, admitting at least to themselves their vulnerability, compare themselves as the result even more unfavourably with their fellow human beings. What may start out as a need to ward off anxiety by convincing others of one's own adequacy may end up as an ability to deceive onself that one is totally invulnerable. Such invulnerability is, however, often bought at the cost of those around one who have to suffer the effects of the insensitivity and egotism that such self-deception needs to maintain itself: for example, the hard, tough man who inflexibly pursues his success and refuses to countenance emotional doubt or weakness in himself may well, if married, have a wife almost screamingly desperate to have herself acknowledged as a person with feelings, but who may have to settle for the role of a silly, weak, inadequate woman who needs his stern and unbending 'protection'.

The chief way of protecting yourself from the basic anxieties which are almost universal in our culture is to develop a pose, or an 'image' behind which you can hide your 'true self'. Such poses are often to be met with: the joker, the hard man, the plain speaker, the martyr, the seducer or seductress, the simple girl, the big bearded teddybear, the dizzy blonde, the battleaxe – the reader will be able to think of many more examples. Most of us develop such images up to a point – indeed it would be hard to get by in the world without one – but difficulties are likely to ensue if people fall for their own images to the extent that their 'true self' disappears. This may be what happens with some people who come to be labelled 'psychotic', but it is probably most easily observable in the case of some so-called 'celebrities' who find themselves almost willy nilly having to live up to the expectations that they themselves have created in bringing themselves to public attention. The 'normal', mythical world in which most of us believe is heavily populated by such unreal figures. I find it interesting that several psychiatrists and psychologists have written about the contrast between the false image and the true self as if the development of the former is an abnormal phenomenon; whatever might have been the case at the time of their writing, it seems to me now that the development of a false image has become the rule rather than the exception. I shall consider this possibility further when looking, in Chapter 3, at the subject of shyness.

Despite our readiness to consider them at, as it were, a distance (for example in literature and popular entertainment), our cultural mythology has it that negative experiences such as psychological anguish, self-doubt, anger and hatred towards others (particularly family members), helplessness and inade-quacy – the kinds of feelings in which 'symptoms' tend to be embedded – are not things which trouble 'normal' people overmuch. And yet the true nature of society is such that it is virtually impossible to get far through life without feeling any or all of these things. But because of our institutional myths, we find when we do feel them that there are very few means at our disposal whereby we might take them seriously. Instead, we are confronted only with standards of how we *ought* to be: our parents should love and protect us and we should love and respect them, we should succeed at school and at work while cooperating amicably with others, we should be sexually 'normal', have happy marriages, love our children, increase and enjoy our material possessions, earn the respect of those with whom we come into contact, and in general conform to what is expected of us in the context of our particular place in society. We are born, it seems, into an absolutely real and unalterable world which cannot be expected to bend as we come up against it, so that we must therefore adapt to it. You may, of course, grow up in a council flat or a stately home, a middle-class suburb or a slum, but whatever your experience you are not likely to see the world as something you can alter.

After a time, you may well become aware that the particular world you occupy departs in some respects from the ideals and values of the wider society, or that you personally do not match up to what seems to be valued: if you are stupid you ought to be clever, if you are poor you ought to be richer, if you are ugly you ought to be beautiful, if you are (at a certain age) single you ought to be married, if you are shy you should be confident, if fat you should be thinner, if skinny you should be plumper, and so on and on. If you fail, as you are bound to do, in these or any other respects, you will find whole armies of professionals ready to iron out the bumps: psychiatrists, psychologists, social workers, educators, religious advisers, cosmetic surgeons, beauticians, accountants, family therapists – the list can be extended indefinitely. In the vast majority of cases the professionals share a common aim – to fit you better into society, not to alter our social institutions so that they will make more comfortable room for you. In other words, when you fail you will find almost no one ready to take your failure seriously, and no conceptual structure, no language, in which to consider it – you will just be exhorted to try even harder to succeed. With a little help from your professional advisers, you will have to bend and distort your already battered image to comply more closely with what is acceptable.

But, of course, however much we do not like to acknowledge

the fact, the very essence of our social organization and cultural ideals demands that there must be a very large proportion of failures. For some people to succeed, others must fail; for one person to be clever, another must be stupid; for a girl to be beautiful, others must be plain. All the time, unremittingly, people are forced to compare themselves with others in terms of what they *are*, that is, in terms of what valuation society places upon them. For every good-looking, assured, rich and powerful man there will be thousands who view him with envy and shame, and struggle the harder to conceal their own implied inadequacy, disguising their hatred when necessary with an outward show of admiration which may even turn eventually to slavish deference. For every tanned, taut-skinned, smooth and lissom girl there will be thousands who look in the mirror at their white, soft, gently bulging bodies with disgust and only just concealed despair.

Our values are not such that they *could* be positively achieved by everybody, or even by most people: they are *bound* to generate failure and distress more than comfort and happiness.

Most people, metaphorically, walk round under the baleful gaze of a relentless judge – the 'generalized other' who measures you with a cold eye and, almost inevitably, finds you wanting. No wonder so many people find themselves, for example, cowering in their homes, sick with dread if they have to venture out into the world beyond their own four walls (and worse, by succumbing to their fear, relegating themselves to a new class of failures – the 'agoraphobics'). And yet, I wonder whether people such as these really are failures, or whether between us we have managed to create a society in which cruelty has got out of hand. It may perhaps be that the person whose anxious dread has shattered the mythical reality in which we are taught to believe has caught on to a truth which the rest of us are desperate not to acknowledge, and for which there are almost no words to provide an understanding.

# 2 The Reality of Threat

The deepest preoccupations and concerns of 'human nature' – or at least, the ways in which they are expressed and experienced – vary with the times and circumstances in which human beings find themselves. For all that we should like to believe otherwise, human beings are not machines whose nature has been fixed once and for all; the 'truth' about people is not static.

My own view of what those preoccupations and concerns are is, then, shaped by the social conditions in which we find ourselves; as times change, so will the preoccupations and concerns. And this is just as well, for if people were to continue to experience themselves as they seem mostly to do now, the future would look very bleak indeed (as it is, only a fool would say that it is rosy).

It is certainly not easy to penetrate behind the mythical world in an attempt to find out why our investment in it is so heavy and so extensive: on the whole, it allows itself to be talked about, so to speak, only in its own terms and in its own myth-creating language. There are very few circumstances available to us in which we can, in good faith, investigate with others the meaning of our experience, the sources of our secret despair. Whether it be with oneself or others, honesty is threatening, and in any case few people are capable of achieving it even if they want to. Honesty breaks through the screen of myth, giving glimpses of a truer world which may be almost unbearably frightening to live in.

This, perhaps, is why psychotherapy as an institution has become a prominent feature of our age. Although, like our other institutions, psychotherapy is used most frequently to strengthen rather than weaken the grip of myth, it does at its best at least afford the possibility of working towards honest communication: it is one of the few arenas in which people can pursue the truth about themselves and their lives without the threat of blame or disapproval, and without risk of hurting or offending the person to whom they are revealing themselves.

It is, then, through my experience of talking to people in psychotherapy that I have caught my own glimpses of what seem to be some of the features of our predicament, of some aspects of the real world behind the myth.

It is perhaps no accident that, as a species, we base our relations with each other on the threat of annihilation, for the preoccupation shown by nations with the nuclear destruction of other nations does no more than give an outer, one might almost say symbolic, form to the threat of annihilation with which most individuals live in their day-to-day lives. This latter is not, to be sure, so much a physical threat as a psychological one – a fate worse than death which, often enough, makes suicide seem preferable.

In order satisfactorily to function, we depend, throughout our lives, on the presence of others who will accord us validity, identity and reality. You cannot *be* anything if you are not *recognized* as something; in this way your being becomes dependent on the regard of somebody else. You may be confirmed, or you may be disconfirmed, and if the latter is the case, often enough and pervasively enough, you simply cease to exist as a person.

*John was an orphan, and had been brought up by an aunt and uncle, only the former of whom had shown him any real warmth. He was shy, and made few friends, though he was an extremely gifted boy who excelled at all sports as well as being academically competent at school. When in his early twenties, he was one day walking along a path in the middle of a small park when he suddenly became terrified that he would float off the face of the earth. He knew, of course, the factual impossibility of this, but nevertheless from that day on became incapable of leaving his home without intolerable feelings of panic. He was unable to go out at all for some years unless accompanied by his wife, and then only with great discomfort.*

In fact, John had had very little experience of confirmation by others, and if, literally as well as metaphorically, he strayed far enough from the gaze of those who had regard for him, the reality of his existence ebbed away, so that he was left floating in empty space.

Even those who move confidently in a relatively secure network of confirming relationships cannot be unfamiliar with the experience of disconfirmation: it must happen to everyone at various points in their lives. Think, for example, of the times when you have openly and innocently exposed your feelings to somebody important to you, only to be met by an icy rebuff which totally misperceives your intentions: for a moment you are enveloped in a sick, acid, freezing loneliness which seems to drain the very blood from your veins. This is the pain worse than all others, and, if experienced in more than occasional small doses, the fate worse than death.

Because we are so dependent on *being* something, and because that must in turn depend on the recognition and confirmation of others, it becomes enormously important to feel *loved*. Love seems to be the prototype confirmation, tangible proof of the acceptance and recognition of what you are, the ultimate approval. I am not sure that this is, so to speak, an eternal verity, but it does seem to me that this is what most people mean by and experience as love in the present age. With a constant supply of love you can go confidently from strength to strength; if the supply is threatened or interrupted, or otherwise in question, you are overcome with anxiety, panic and dread; without it, you cease to exist as a real person, but may live a false, defended life in which pain is never far from the surface.

This means that love is not simply a positive experience, something that may be relied on in some circumstances (for example in families) and welcomed as a nice surprise in others (for example courtship), something which makes the world a nice, brighter place. It makes of love, in fact, a most terrible weapon which can be used to confirm or annihilate, to blackmail or torture as well as to cherish and nurture. The threat with which we live is the threat of not being loved.

*Richard has been dealt a number of unusually unkind blows by fate in the course of his life. Most of these he deals with courageously and energetically, but sometimes his confidence collapses and he gives way to states of anxious panic which he experiences as physical illness. He remembers how, as a child, he used to fear that, every time he left the house, his parents would fetch another little boy from the attic whom they loved much more than him.*

*Anne felt her mother's hatred so much that she used as a child to comfort herself with the fantasy that perhaps she was an orphan whose parents would really have loved her (at the time, of course, she would not have been able to put it in quite these words). Her unusual ability to see her early experience so clearly is perhaps what enables her now to take a remarkably brave and constructive grip on her life, even if she pursues her aims in great fear and trembling.*

It is not surprising that most forms of psychotherapy concentrate at some point on early childhood experience, for it is of course in relation to one's parents (or substitute parents) that one first gains an idea of what one is, and of whether that 'self' is or is not lovable. People's fundamental feelings about their self-worth take shape throughout childhood as they become aware of what they are worth to those closest to them (usually, of course, parents).

Our mythical culture takes it more or less for granted that parents love their children (those who betray the myth too grossly – and usually get the social services into trouble as well – invoke our most extreme self-righteous horror), but as a generality this seems to be far from the case, unless, that is, one can see love as coming in some very strange disguises. It is of course true that many parents feel intensely bound up with their children, but too often affection is conditional on the child's conforming to parental needs and expectations, and its withdrawal can at any moment project the child into the cold isolation which threatens to nullify its existence.

Many parents are so in need themselves of the kind of nurturing confirmation they know they should give to their children that the latter simply become competitors, and some parents are certainly unprepared for the demands children will make on them, find their offspring exhausting and draining, and are unable to meet their needs. This is bound to be the case at some times with all parents, and yet many become extremely guilty and anxious at discovering how irritable and destructive they are capable of feeling towards their children. Others simply give vent to their irritation.

*Kathleen is a lonely woman, longing for the warmth and support of the people she left behind in Ireland (though her large family was not particularly affectionate). Her husband is a self-employed builder who works most weekends and evenings and can no longer bear to listen to her complaints of homesickness. She has no real friends on the estate where they live, finding the people cold and spiteful. She gets her main comfort from drinking, which is beginning to get a grip on her. One evening after she was supposed to be in bed, Kathleen's three-year-old daughter came down the stairs asking for a glass of milk. Kathleen, interrupted in her lonely relationship with a pint of cheap sherry, found herself beside herself with rage, screaming hysterically at her daughter, and hurling a bottle of milk to smash against the wall not far from the girl's head. She was so frightened and ashamed by this episode, which she dared not confess to her husband, that she forced herself to confide in her doctor.*

For many people, children quickly become allies or enemies in the unhappy battles they are waging with their husbands or wives. Countless fathers, for example, find themselves eased out of the family circle (often into the potting shed, the garage, or the pub) while their children became instructed by their mother in what beasts men are (male children brought up in this regime often develop into fastidious, anxious men who have a kind of disgust for all things masculine, which of course makes their own lives very difficult to lead; female children from such a background often have an instinctive loathing and contempt for men which they themselves find hard to understand). Because so many men in our culture are heavily defended against any kind of emotional sensitivity (betraying, perhaps, a tacit knowledge of the dreadful risks to which their need for love exposes them), their wives often feel neglected, misunderstood, lonely and anxious, and their daughters fail to learn what really goes on underneath the male façade, so that they later relate to men on models they have perforce had to construct from fantasy. Such men are often particularly intensely threatened by love in all its aspects, and fend it off with, at best, distance and indifference and, at worst, brutality: their daughters may become anxious, submissive and profoundly lacking in confidence, their sons defensive and uncertain.

Many parents are made intensely anxious by any sign that their children are developing in ways which do not conform to their expectations and (usually implicit and unexamined) values. A child may find itself hated simply because it looks like a relative who is disliked or found threatening by either or both of its parents. Coercion, ranging from the periodic withdrawal of affection to full-blown assault and battery, is a ubiquitous feature of parent-child relations, and children quickly learn to distort themselves to fit expectations if they are not to be thrown, as it were, into outer darkness. Particularly in middle-class families, positive parental expectations can place enormous stress upon their children – they must be clever, do well at school, harbour no unrefined thoughts or feelings, become doctors or lawyers, etc.: again, the manipulative use of love is the weapon which works towards the desired result.

In families with several children, the latter often come to

occupy well defined roles, any departure from which on their part is met with instant disconfirmation and rejection. There are many girls, for example, who come to occupy the 'Cinderella' role: the less pretty daughter with the heart of gold who becomes the family drudge, the one who always helps the others, takes responsibility, keeps her expectation of personal success and happiness low (and ends up with a bleak life of service to others). If, in the family, she makes any attempt to establish a more satisfying place for herself, she is made to feel that her golden heart has turned to stone, that she is becoming corrupted by selfishness and getting above herself; in later life her internalization of these values means that she is unable to please herself without feeling overwhelming anxiety and guilt.

The control of children through the withdrawal of love happens in the subtlest of ways, and is usually denied by the parents at any explicit level – their own anxiety does not permit them to see what they are doing. Many children are brought up in an emotional world which is structured by magic: control is exercised by hints and hidden threats, in which punishment is somehow transmitted by non-human powers, and any attempt at rebellion is likely to be met with a kind of blast of superstitious dread.

*Jane, an only child, spent her entire childhood being overwhelmed by her parents' assurances of their love for her, and they were zealous in attending to her every want. Anger and hatred were not allowed in her household. Her mother spent a lot of time consulting horoscopes and spiritualist manuals, and the family's life was ruled by the never quite expressed necessity for warding off the powers of evil. One of Jane's memories, which she could make no sense of, is of taking a Christmas present from her mother upstairs and, secretly, jumping on it. In her early adult life she became troubled by obsessional fears that she could harm people by wishing them ill, which she found herself doing compulsively. What worried her most was that her evil wishes were always directed at those whom she loved most, like her mother for instance.*

Parents can do the most appalling things to their children out of their concern for them.

*After a row with her father when she was fifteen, May stormed out of the house and walked round the park for, for her, an unusually long time. When she got back after dark, her father, beside himself with anger and anxiety, dragged her down to the doctor demanding that he examine her to see if her virginity was still intact.*

People, on the whole, are not aware of the extent to which they have been blackmailed, coerced, distorted and subdued by the many uses to which 'love' and its withdrawal can be put. For most individuals, their experience is simply their experience, and certainly as children they had no way of knowing that things might have been different. Even people whose childhood has been one long history of neglect and rejection (a much more frequent feature of our world than we like to think) often speak respectfully of their parents and see themselves as having had a reasonably normal and even happy childhood. At first, the link between their lack of confidence and feelings of worthlessness on the one hand and their childhood experience on the other is hard for them to see. We tend to take it for granted that what we experienced from our parents as children is what is meant by parental love.

It is difficult for anybody who takes the trouble to inquire into the backgrounds of people in distress not to become angry with parents. There is no doubt that family life is frequently a scene of horrific violence – more often subtle and psychological than overt and physical – and it seems unforgivable that morally responsible adults could inflict the kinds of things they do on their innocent offspring. And yet, of course, the victims become themselves parents, and in all probability perpetrate similar violence on their own children. We tend to blame only those we have not taken the trouble to understand. I can sympathize with Mrs X who tells me how she hit her daughter – can even encourage her not to feel too bad about it – because I also know that she is coping with an unemployed and alcoholic husband and an overcrowded council flat with noisy and aggressive neighbours. It is therefore foolish of me to feel righteous anger when she tells me how her father used regularly and for no apparent reason to belt her until she bled even up to the age of seventeen, when she ran away to get married. Such relationships are not due simply to the wickedness of individuals, but take place in a cultural setting which makes our (mythical) ideals hard to achieve.

However, our experience as individuals starts at a given point, and a purely sociological analysis leaves us personally untouched as we struggle to understand what has happened to us and how we are to deal with it. The relations between parents and children, the corrupted love which threatens annihilation, indeed sets up a vicious circle in which the apportionment of blame is irrelevant, but as people we can approach the problem personally only from our particular vantage point. For most individuals, their first experience of the 'other', the remorseless judge who may bestow or withdraw confirmation, is personified in their parents.

There are of course those who conclude that the 'nuclear family' is an inevitable source of oppression and exploitation, and that human relations would be better learned in other kinds of nursery. Although I am sure that what happens in families is by no means unrelated to the culture beyond them (in ways some of which we shall consider later), this does not seem to me an argument for their abolition. That love is abused is no reason for dismantling its most effective cradle. It is the very powerfulness of love which makes it so dangerous, and it seems to me preferable to try to understand the ways in which it is misused rather than to get rid of it altogether.

The greatest misuse to which we put love, I believe, is to make it the conditional ground on which people can *be* rather than the unconditional ground from which they can *do*: we love people as objects rather than subjects. Love has become a certain kind of approval, the bestowal of confirmation or disconfirmation on people who meet or fail to meet certain objective criteria. As others have pointed out, children quickly get an idea of themselves as having certain kinds of 'selves' which are describable in terms of either approving or disapproving labels. John *is* clever, or brave, or naughty or strong; Jane *is* pretty, or wilful, or silly, or delicate. With the partial exception of physical labels, which have implications to be considered in a later chapter, these words are misapplied. Only actions can be clever or stupid, brave or cowardly, good or bad, etc. What I do stupidly today I might do cleverly tomorrow, but I shall find it more difficult if I have already accepted the label 'stupid' – I may well find, indeed, that it is more important to live up to the label than to risk disconfirmation by stepping out of role. We have to earn the love of those who are important to us by becoming the objects they wish us to be.

Sometimes it may lie within a child's possibilities to become what its parents want it to be, and it may conform, most often not without strain, but sometimes glowing with satisfaction and confidence at the confirming approval this brings: in this case the child ends up with a validated 'sense of self', a clear, self-conscious picture of the kind of person he or she has become, frequently not untainted by a kind of self-congratulatory bumptiousness which is unlikely to be punctured just because people take exception to it.

Many children, however, are in some or many important respects unable to fulfil the expectations of their parents, and carry round with them, so to speak, raw, painful areas of disconfirmation which leave them exposed to sudden attacks of self-doubt and uncertainty, sudden ebbings of self-confidence which may well be experienced as 'symptoms' of anxiety or depression.

*Annette remembers vividly a day when, at the age of about six or so, she was playing a solitary skipping game in the back yard, and accompanying it with a song she had learned at school, the words of which she has since realized are mildly obscene. Suddenly her mother stormed out of the back door, hit her hard across the face, and ordered her to bed. In retrospect, Annette can see why her mother reacted as she did, though at the time she gave her daughter no explanation. One of Annette's 'symptoms' is to fear that people will think her stupid or bad if she talks or acts spontaneously in public, and consequently she is mildly 'agoraphobic'.*

It would of course be foolish to suggest that one such incident as this could determine the future course of someone's experience. The significance of the memory lies rather in pointing to what might have been (indeed, in view of other evidence which there is little need to spell out here, probably was) a pervasive state of affairs in this person's childhood.

Because they are disconfirmed as people (objects), it is natural for children to conclude that they are in some way flawed 'selves', they do not come up to scratch in certain essential respects: they are, quite simply, in some ways unlovable. The child does not as a rule criticize its parents' conception of it; understandably, the parental view is accepted by the child as the one which accurately mediates reality. If the child is unloved, it must be because it is unlovable. Even as adults with quite clearly elaborated concepts of right and wrong and good and bad, and who are able to see – in others – what does and does not constitute adequate child-rearing practice, there are many people who cannot actually experience their own quite often horrendous treatment as children as having been anything but their 'own fault'. If their parents treated them badly it must have been because, despite their best efforts, they could not overcome their children's unlovableness sufficiently to love them. Under the surface feelings of anxiety or panic, then, there is often a self-loathing which seems the appropriate response to what the person has learned about him- or herself from an apparently objective parental assessment. Often, people are reluctant to expose themselves to any experience which might suggest that they are worth more than they think they are, as if it becomes more comfortable to live in the role assigned to you than to risk an even worse fate by rebelling against it. I can think, for example, of many women whose (in particular) fathers conveyed, whatever they actually felt, little more than hatred towards them, who move from one degrading and pain-filled relationship with men to another, with very little hope and a great deal of despair, and yet who even consciously reject more promising-looking relationships on the grounds that they 'don't deserve' them.

Love is the stamp of approval on an objective 'self', but rarely is the approval total, and life may at any moment throw up circumstances which expose those raw and unconfirmed aspects of ourselves which we shamefully hide from the public gaze. Since we have no articulate understanding of our condition, we experience such moments as the incomprehensible onslaught of anxiety: a symptomatic attack which appears 'out of the blue'. We go through life like commodities on a conveyor belt, being probed by some electronic eye for flaws, with the rubber stamp 'reject' ever poised to fall upon us should such a flaw be found.

The 'other' thus becomes a terrible threat as well as a potential saviour: we depend for our self-confidence and well-being on the endorsement of the other and yet we are just as likely to be annihilated by him or her.

The parent as 'other' is, as it were, its first and most powerful instance, but clearly almost anyone else can occupy its place in the individual's experience. As you go through life you are assessed, docketed and judged according to an ever-widening range of criteria – at home, at school, at work, at leisure, by family and friends, teachers and colleagues: you fall almost continuously under an evaluating, objectifying gaze. It can surely be no accident that anxiety is so often experienced by people when they are, literally, exposed to the gaze of others. So-called 'agoraphobia' is rarely experienced by people as a fear of open spaces – indeed, many 'agoraphobics' feel quite comfortable walking alone on deserted roads or in the open countryside, in fog or in the dark. It is in crowded places – shops and buses, busy streets, restaurants, parties and other social gatherings, where the real panic usually strikes. Most people who experience this kind of anxiety, which can be excruciatingly painful and frightening, readily make the connexion between fear and social exposure when they are offered it, but not so many make it for themselves: at first, often, the 'symptoms' are seen as inexplicable, indicative perhaps of some kind of physical illness. While people may be able to say that they are afraid of making a public spectacle of themselves in some way, for example by passing out on a bus or vomiting in a restaurant, the concept of simply fearing the gaze of the 'other' is not one which makes immediate sense to the average Anglo-Saxon mind. If you are afraid, it is thought, it must be of something specific, if you are worrying, you must be worrying about a 'problem' – it does not seem reasonable to suggest that fear can be a state of being. This is perhaps how some people are able to deceive themselves about the meaning of their sensations – it cannot be fear, they argue, because there is nothing immediately present which could reasonably give rise to fear; the sensations must therefore be signs of illness.

Usually, of course, vulnerability to the generalized gaze of the 'other' – to strangers in a supermarket, even to faceless windows in a street – is not in itself a total 'explanation'. The person's confidence, belief in him- or herself as a satisfactory object, has been initially sapped in some other context, usually parental, often, secondarily, marital. But the way the dread of annihilation takes us, the panicky feeling of strangeness and the ebbing away of one's familiar existence (sometimes called 'depersonalization' by psychiatrists) is indicative of something much wider than our personal weaknesses and failures: it is the negative aspect of a way of life to which we all subscribe, the price we pay for objectifying each other under our mutual gaze. Under that gaze we freeze and tremble, flush and stammer because we know full well, and utterly realistically, what it can do to us: it can annihilate us.

The dependence on the other for confirmation renders every relationship in which the other features (that is, as things are, just about every relationship) fraught with awful danger.

'Loving' relationships become secret, undercurrent battle-grounds, in which we stalk each other warily sniffing the atmosphere for indications of rejection. To allow yourself to be loved by another is to put yourself totally in his or her power, to hand him or her the means of your destruction, because, by and large, we love one another only as objects (it may not be without significance that a leading school of depth psychology sees love as an aspect of 'object relations', indeed, is known as the 'object relations school').

Though objectifying confirmation and disconfirmation is a ubiquitous feature of our social organization, nowhere is the dangerousness of the risks we run in 'loving' more evident than in the relations of men with women and women with men. Perhaps it is the very 'otherness' of the opposite sex which makes the acceptance and confirmation of one of its members so initially warming and rewarding – for example in the (re-latively rare) experience of 'falling in love'. However, the fact that, even when it does occur in its most florid form, this state of relationship never seems to last all that long suggests that for people to live and move and have their being in each other places a strain on their capacities to meet each other's needs which only almost superhuman generosity on each individual's part can overcome. Sooner or later the lover's needs take prece-dence over those of the beloved, and that is the point at which they will discover whether a continued relationship – as, as it were, consenting adults who can accept a measure of their own aloneness – is possible. The greater the dependence of one partner on another, the greater the likelihood that he or she will end up feeling bitterly rejected.

It is certainly no accident that so many people who are overcome by 'symptoms' of anxiety acute enough for them to seek professional help are relatively young women with small children, cut off from close contact with their own families, and dependent for the survival of their identity on husbands who have changed from being attentive lovers to near-strangers who come home late, tired from work, and unwilling to talk about anything. No longer confirmed under the loving gaze of any 'significant other', trapped in a form of drudgery which is these days no longer socially valued, such women find them-selves additionally drained by the demands of their own child-ren who call upon resources for love and attention which seem rapidly to be running dry. Even in spite of the current raised consciousness of feminist principles (which seem not to have penetrated far beyond the orbit of those relatively liberated and independent women who have least need of them) our cultural mythology has it that this kind of situation is utterly 'normal' and desirable, so that women who find themselves in it have, so to speak, no critical purchase upon it: if they feel unhappy, anxious and unreal, it must be because they are either 'ill' or 'inadequate', and if they detect in themselves feelings of destructive violence towards their children (a not uncommon 'symptom' consequent upon their depleted ability to meet their children's needs) their alarm and guilt may quickly drive them to their doctor. Since sexuality is so responsive to the relational context in which it is set, it is very often also the case that women in such circumstances find themselves less eager than they once were to make love to their uncommunicative husbands, and frequently they experience this as a puzzling and alarming development.

It is easy to cast men in the role of villain in these circumstances. But they have their problems too. Focused on breadwinning, unaware that many of their needs for confirmation may be being met to some extent through their relations with people at work, they are confused and irritated by their wives' demands on them (cannot see the nature of their underlying needs), and become hurt and angry to find that the validating sexual warmth which satisfied their most fundamental need for confirmation (as well as their lust, which is all that their wives by now can see) is no longer half so readily available. Eventually, nursing their pain behind a wall of feigned (or self-deceiving) indifference, they retire into the back room with their personal computers, or into a shed in the back yard with their rabbits or their CB radios. This, certainly, may not be the world as presented to us by the colour supplements, but it is much more real.

In the arena of male–female relations there are many variations on this theme, but the major components are usually not dissimilar to those sketched out above. The reasons for this state of affairs are no doubt complex and manifold, stretching through individuals' personal histories out into the culture beyond and the socially determined roles which men and women are expected to adopt. No doubt to a significant extent it is a man's world, and perhaps for the most part men are better placed to survive some of its more painful demands, but for one sex simply to blame the other would be to miss one central and very important point, and to decrease the chances of men and women understanding each other. The point is that to depend on the 'other' – in this case the sexual partner – for confirmation of one's being is bound to lead to disconfirming annihilation, because such a demand can only be met through a self-denying generosity and sacrifice on the other's part which is beyond the competence of ordinary mortals. Once the dependency is created, the confirmation supplied and then withdrawn, the loved and loving other becomes the hated and annihilating other, and men and women find themselves opposing each other with bristling hostility and contempt. Our very 'selves' have become objectified commodities in an emotional marketplace, and, having lost the freedom of our subjectivity, we are at the mercy of those others who may choose us or reject us, purchase or replace us, install us at the warmth of their hearth, or leave us on the shelves.

One does not have to be a psychotherapist to see everywhere evidence of the pain that men and women inflict on each other and themselves. For example, having failed once to extort the necessary confirmation from their partner, or having received it for only a relatively fleeting period, people may of course embark, through a series of either actual or fantasized affairs, on a search for it elsewhere (this seems to be the particular, if by no means the sole province of the middle-aged). The initial reassuring warmth of a new sexual liaison is something that can be endlessly repeated but rarely emotionally consummated. For women with children whose freedom of action is more limited, many sad hours may be spent in daydreams of a rescuing knight. One only has to glance at the popular literature designed for women and young girls to see how far our culture still offers them salvation as the handmaidens of men, where all they have to do to earn undying faithfulness is love and serve. For men, the passionate submission of a series of otherwise aloof, sultry and sexy (though emotionally undemanding) young women is supposed to be what will charge their batteries sufficiently for them to conquer the world. Trite as these myths are, one detects them over and over again in the fantasies which fuel people's hopes, and sometimes guide their actions, while they drive each other to despair. There are also, of course, those whose experience of parental attitudes and strife has determined them, albeit unawares, never to enter the fray themselves, so that their sexuality becomes attached to safer 'objects', and they find themselves, like electronic machines, being 'turned on' by a wide range of stimuli which need not necessarily have anything much to do with other people at all.

The all-pervasive threat of annihilation means that we have to armour ourselves against the dangers of relationship, cultivate an indifference towards tenderness so that we are anaesthetized to the pain its withdrawal can inflict. Our fear of loving and being loved is apparent at every level of our social existence, from the personal to the institutional. Karen Horney, a psychoanalyst of great distinction whose major work was carried out towards the end of the first half of this century, pointed out that a fundamental strategy of 'neurosis' is to seek security rather than satisfaction. Thirty or so years later, this now seems to be almost everyone's central preoccupation, and, indeed, forms the major rationale even for international relations. Our concern is not to betray our vulnerability, not to become 'exposed' (perhaps this is why, at the national level, 'spies' are singled out for particular vituperation and especially savage punishment, and why, at the level of popular culture, espionage seems so fascinating). It certainly seems hardly questionable that the 'denial of tenderness' is a predominantly male phenomenon, and it is undoubtedly the case that many men who seek professional help with 'symptoms' of anxiety which seem to be getting out of hand are in fact paying the price for developing such a rigidly tough posture towards the world that the defence starts to crack and their relationships with those important to them start to disintegrate in a way which exposes their tender foundations. Frequently also, men find that they simply cannot keep up with the demands for toughness that their role seems to make of them: they feel weak, effeminate, silly and useless. But defensiveness is not a purely male prerogative, and we shall be considering later other ways in which we try to ward off the worst threats to which we are exposed by our objectified existence, as well as some of the costs we incur thereby in terms of crippling our capacity for creative, subjective existence and less destructive relationships.

One cannot comfortably go through life with a continuous awareness of the threat of annihilation under which one lives. Just as one cannot, without succumbing to despair, hold in one's mind for long the extent of the largely unseen apparatus we have painstakingly built for the destruction of our planet, so one cannot live with a continuous conscious examination of the ways in which we threaten each other psychologically: we conduct our lives within our defences, largely unconscious that they exist, and taking for granted the ways we relate (or fail to relate) to each other as features of an unalterable reality. Like well defended space craft, we find the painful and destructive rays we direct at each other bouncing off our hardened shells as we cruise aimlessly through a life-space structured as much by market forces and technical 'progress' as by any human purpose of our own. Every so often a shot penetrates, and, because he or she has failed to develop the requisite armour, a person disintegrates like a dot on a space invaders screen. Because defensiveness has become the norm, the medium in which we live, we notice its presence no more than a fish notices the water it swims in, but pretend rather to be guided by the mythical values we see as 'objectively' established around us. We have no language with which to comment upon our true predicament, but experience it inarticulately through our 'symptoms' and our dread.

# 3 Shyness and the Self as Object

It is almost impossible, in our culture, not to be self-conscious –
that is, aware of oneself as being under the gaze of others, of
being evaluated by them and vulnerable to rejection by them.
We do not define *ourselves* as people, but are defined by those
with whom we come into contact, and it is our awareness of
their opinion of us which furnishes our consciousness of self.

Very early on – most probably from our parents – we start to
get an idea of ourselves as being this, that or the other 'kind' of
person, we discover (so it seems) that we have 'selves' which are
describable in certain more or less definite terms. We cannot, as
things are, escape the definitions which are imposed upon us,
nor find a way to make ourselves immune to the ever-present
threat of having a negative, rejecting judgment passed upon us.
The person who professes not to care what others think of him,
but rather to rest content in his confidence in his own worth, is
simply deceiving himself: as long as one claims to *be* anything,
the claim must in the final analysis depend on the endorsement
of others if it is to be valid.

The processes whereby we, as it were, negotiate what kind of
objectification will eventually be imposed upon us are, however,
extremely complex and subtle, and, because they are not in
themselves objective, are largely opaque to our inspection: if
challenged, we would probably deny that we were engaged in
such processes at all. Yet it is obvious from even the most
everyday interactions between people that everyone has very
sophisticated ways of coping with others, ways which imply
some kind of awareness (even if it would be impossible to put it
into words) of the difficulties and dangers to self-esteem involved in our relations with each other. Even a simple greeting
between neighbours, or a chance conversation in a bus queue,
can convey enormous amounts of information about what each
participant thinks of the other, and about how they would *like*
to be thought of. The skill and subtlety which people display in
relating to each other even in such unimportant encounters as
these suggests that everyone is a psychologist, both in the
sense of having a highly developed practical ability to deal with
other people and in the sense of having an implicit theory about
the reasons why people conduct themselves as they do: even
if we cannot say how we do it, we show by and large great
ingenuity in negotiating the relational dangers of everyday

life. In order successfully to carry out these interpersonal operations, so to speak, we must rely on the most subtle and fleeting of 'cues', placing our bets on the kind of 'subjective' evidence which no self-respecting professional psychologist would touch with a barge pole. Indeed, it is almost impossible to say how one reaches the intuitions one does about other people – how, for example, one knows the difference between a true and a fake smile, catches the flash of anxiety in somebody's eye, becomes aware of a current of sexual interest between two total strangers who have only just met.

This kind of sensitivity, infinitely finer and more accurate than any of the crudely obvious insights offered by the 'body language' analysts, is, I believe, present in just about every-body, though people vary greatly in the extent to which they are willing to place their trust in it. It gives us access to a world we all share, just as our physical senses (because, presumably, of the similarity in physical structure between our bodies) give us access to a natural world about which we have built up a huge and complex (scientific) shared understanding. This is a theme which will be developed in greater detail towards the end of this book.

The world to which our intuitive sensitivity gives us access is the intricate and finely balanced subjective world in which we conduct our relations with each other, register and react to the impressions we give and receive, administer and respond to offers of love or threats of annihilation. Because of the enor-mous delicacy involved in our dealings with each other in these respects, and because of the extreme dangers inherent in them, we do not normally comment upon what we are up to: lan-guage, it seems, is far too crude to be allowed, as it were, to clothe our transactions in the coarse obviousness of words. Words objectify and make concrete what we seem to prefer to keep as a screened, fluid sensitivity which does not have to answer for its insights and actions, keep to its promises, or meet the crass demands of logical analysis. And yet we rely on this unexamined and mercurial faculty to tell us the truth about what is going on between us far more than on the verbal accounts we give each other and ourselves as 'explanations' and excuses. Indeed, were we to rely on our *explicit* psychological theories – whether lay or professional – for the conduct of our social life, we should find it virtually impossible to maintain any semblance of order or predictability in our dealings with each other, and would spend much of the time laboriously trying to work out what was happening with the aid of a totally inadequate vocabulary.

The psychotherapist, certainly, would get nowhere without a heavy reliance on the accuracy of his or her intuitive understanding of patients, since very often what patients are prepared to say about themselves is very far indeed from being the case. And it is only because the therapist knows (trusts) that the patient *shares* the categories of understanding yielded by intuition that he or she is able to appeal to the patient's good faith (i.e. abandonment in the safety of the therapeutic relationship of the possibilities for deception offered by language) so that the truth may be acknowledged.

There is nothing special in these respects about psychotherapists and their patients. The immediate knowledge of interpersonal 'truth' afforded by intuitive sensitivity and the possibilities for obscuring it inherent in language are universal phenomena.

It is not that the heavy hand of 'scientific psychology' has not attempted to grasp this faculty and render it amenable to objective inspection. Through ponderous analyses of eye-contact, gesture, facial expression and other 'objective', 'behavioural' indices, psychologists have hoped to be able to make 'predictable' and 'controllable' the last vestiges of our subjectivity. But even in so far as this project appears to succeed (so that, for example, salesmen, 'communicators' and the socially withdrawn may be able to be trained in the secrets of 'body language') it simply renders even more recondite and invisible the springs of our subjectivity as we learn that we can no longer trust the 'behavioural cues' which formerly gave us a glimpse of our intentions. It is, therefore, a mistake to suppose that the hidden 'I' which enacts our conduct can ever be made available to objective analysis or 'scientific' description, and the attempt so to make it only widens further the arena in which we can deceive ourselves and each other.

In terms of the considerations raised in earlier chapters, intuitive sensitivity is the faculty whereby we cope with the 'real' world of dangerous and threatening relationships, and language the faculty which mediates the mythical, 'objective' world which we would all much prefer to believe in. Depending on the heaviness of a person's stake in the mythical world, it is entirely possible for him or her to disclaim any trust in or respect for the knowledge which intuitive sensitivity makes available – to disconfirm it, that is, in either the self, or others, or both.

Both as a society and as individuals, it seems to me, our
insistence on preserving our myths at all costs and defending
ourselves from the painful realities of our social lives and their
inherent threat of annihilation, means that we have become
increasingly concerned to deny the evidence, if not of our own
senses (though, perhaps, that is what it comes down to), then at
least of our own sensitivity. (The very fact that I am driven to
use such a clumsily unsatisfactory term as 'intuitive sensitivity'
shows how impoverished is our conceptual apparatus for the
understanding of this faculty.) Most people simply deny what
at another level they know to be the case, or suffer agonies of
indecision over whether to trust their experience or not. In-
terestingly, there is a minority of people who seem to find it
impossible *not* to trust the experience which their intuitive
sensitivity gives them, even though they would much rather
abandon it: they would rather not have the pain of knowing the
truth, but cannot seem to find the secret of escape from it which
others have so easily developed.

A patient asked me recently whether I thought his wife
really did love him. How can one answer such a question?
However complete the behavioural catalogue one could build
up on what she did and did not do for him, one could never be
certain that his description was accurate or that she was not
simply a good dissembler. His question, in fact, was asked out of
utter despair, indicating really that he could no longer trust
himself to judge his own experience: nobody can know (in the
sense of objective certainty) what he wanted me to tell him,
they can only trust what they sense – there is no other court of
appeal in the final analysis. It is of course the false promise of
objectivity to give us 'proofs' of our world which rest on an
authority (for example that of 'Science') more trustworthy than
our own frail powers of perception and reason; indeed, objectivity warns us with all the solemnity which can be mustered by
its collective institutions of the dire perils we run if we are so
foolhardy as to trust our own judgment. Small wonder, then,
that in the case of my patient (who was in fact struggling with
the dawning awareness that his wife did *not* really love him)
reliance on his own experience seemed an impossibly risky
undertaking, so that he sought the 'objectivity' of my view. He
might as reasonably have asked me if the desk between us was
really there (indeed, more reasonably, since at least the desk,
unlike his wife, formed part of my experience as well as his).
There are occasions, beloved of philosophers, when it might

make sense to check with another whether one's experience (even of so well established an object as a desk) is shared, but even this is no objective guarantee of its validity – that judgment remains ultimately and irrevocably personal and subjective.

This is not to say that intuitive sensitivity is infallible – perhaps in part because of the degree to which it has been spurned and ignored in our culture and consequently is as a faculty poorly understood and weakly developed from a conceptual standpoint, it is quite easily put in the service of self-deception. Even so, it is, in the last resort, all we have to go on.

The main escape route offered by our culture from the uncertainties which our sensitivity reveals to us is, then, via objectivity. The more we can turn ourselves into objects (preferably machines) the less attention we need pay to the painful subtleties of our interaction with each other, and the more we can abandon our own experience in favour of a set of socially determined myths which clearly delineate our place in the world and the ways in which we may relate to each other.

Our, as it were, 'official' psychology tells us that we consist of 'selves' which are in turn collections of more or less fixed definable attributes, describable in terms of their relative value along a number of identifiable dimensions. One of psychology's central concerns is thus to establish what characteristics people 'have' (i.e., possess as fixed qualities) and to 'measure' their relative strength or weakness. In this way, it is felt, psychology can be 'scientific', that is, can describe features of human 'personality' and endow them with dimensions which can be measured as if they were objects in physical space. By taking this approach, it is hoped that psychology – in this instance the psychology of personality – might achieve the same sort of success as that achieved by the natural sciences like physics and chemistry in the mastery of inanimate matter, but in this case in the mastery (in particular the 'prediction and control') of human 'behaviour'. Because, so the reasoning goes, natural science is among other things 'objective', and relies heavily on numerical measurement, so psychology must adopt the same standards if it is to gain scientific respectability.

Both science as a whole, and psychology in particular, are of course integral parts of our culture, and as such it is important to remember that they meet the needs we feel and tackle the tasks we set them. However much some of them might like to be, and however much they are seen as such by many people, scientists and psychologists are not creators of our culture, discoverers of ultimate truths which then shape our view of the world, but rather interpreters and refiners of our most fundamental concepts and understandings (and myths). Thus 'official' psychology's most heavy investment seems to be in the kind of 'objectification' of human beings which I argue leads often to the exacerbation of some kinds of psychological distress, but does strengthen defences against the recognition of our real and fundamental vulnerability. The psychologist, with his tests and techniques (often grandiosely called 'measuring instruments'), his power to label and categorize, becomes the very personification of the cold gaze of the Other. For the psychologist the mysteries of human nature have in principle been solved, the general scheme of things is established, and it becomes only a question of how to fit the individual most accurately into his or her allotted slot; no longer is there any need to face the agonizing uncertainties which arise out of human beings' relations with each other as they struggle to evolve a social order and a satisfactory conception of human nature (it is precisely this *evolutionary* nature of psychological phenomena, which by definition can have no final end point, which psychology fails to take account of).

The ways in which we bring about our own objectification are thrown into sharp relief through an examination of the psychological test catalogue of Britain's leading publisher of psychological 'measuring instruments'. Such tests are developed by psychologists, commercially published, and made available for purchase only to suitably qualified 'experts' – clearly, if people are to be restricted to their role as objects they must not be allowed to have access to the means whereby their dimensions can be measured; this is an interesting, if tacit, admission by psychologists that the objects of their study are not really objects at all, for if they were there would be little danger of their tampering with their own dimensions in such a way as to make their measurement inaccurate, and consequently little need to keep the means of measurement a closely guarded secret from them. There are in the catalogue many tests which focus on intelligence and other cognitive 'skills' related to memory, perceptual ability, and so on. These 'skills' are thus 'scientifically' established as possessed by people in finite, measurable amounts, and people may be ordered and categorized relative to each other according to the degree to which they possess them. This obviously has very practical consequences in terms of assigning people to particular strata in educational and vocational settings, much as physical objects could be sorted and graded according, for example, to their size and weight. Should people possess qualities which are not stably measurable in the way insisted upon by psychologists, or which are of no interest to, or have simply been overlooked by them, these will of course remain unappreciated and untapped. As well as intelligence and cognitive 'skills', there are many 'dimensions' of 'personality' which have become the focus of psychological testing. A cursory glance at the catalogue shows that you may, for example, be categorized according to the degree to which you are: submissive, hostile, emotional, masculine/feminine, self-sufficient, introverted/extraverted, sociable, anxious, aggressive, creative, controlling, affectionate, cooperative, stable, competitive, confident, mature, healthy, conforming, conscientious, neurotic, independent, depressed, evasive, exuberant, realistic, conservative. To name but a few.

But what possible sense can it make to endow a person with, for example, the characteristic 'affectionate'? *People* are not affectionate, though their *conduct* might be. Of a *person* one would have to ask *when* is he or she affectionate? With whom? In what circumstances? Under what conditions? Where? In what respects? And the same is true of pretty well all the attributes by means of which this approach attempts to objectify people. Hidden behind this approach is the production-line mentality of our culture, the unquestioned assumption that human beings are to be packaged and graded and valued in the same way as the other, inanimate goods which we learn to covet. Very prominently, the competitiveness of our social organization is evident as a shaping influence on the ways in which we characterize ourselves – what you are is scarcely conceivable except in terms of how you compare with others. There is virtually no room here for the subjectivity of the person, although, of course, our subjectivity is at work behind the scenes in constructing this kind of picture of our world, and in this example is, as it were, temporarily invested in the psychologists whom we appoint to choose for us how we shall be described as objects.

It is no accident that a central concern of social psychology is with 'self-presentation' and 'impression management'. Social psychologists recognize, accurately enough, that you are what you manage to persuade others to take you as: you cannot validly claim to *be* something which the 'significant others' around you repudiate. What one *is* thus becomes a matter of social transaction, and this in turn inevitably breeds a technology of manipulation and deceit in which the plausibility of the front you manage to present becomes all-important. This brand of social psychology reports faithfully enough on the way things are, and does its best (through 'social skills training', etc.) to make life easier for some of those who have difficulty in coming to terms with some of the more brutal aspects of social existence. What it does *not* concern itself with is the philosophical and moral validity of this view of 'being' – above all it does not question (as, for example, has been done in existentialist philosophy) whether it is in itself legitimate to see human beings as 'being' anything. As long as we take for granted an objectifying culture and its materialistic and mechanistic principles, we quite naturally arrive at a 'reality' in which the essence of human relations lies in manipulation, exploitation, deception and competition. If, however, we took account of our subjectivity (which remains submerged and inarticulate in an objectifying culture) we might have to recognize that, though a person may *do* things in ways which can be described as having this or that effect or value, he or she cannot reasonably be described as 'being' anything in particular. In other words, it may not in fact make much sense to talk about people as *having* 'selves' – in the sense of objectively determinable or describable collections of characteristics – at all. This is not to say that people may not conduct themselves in relatively consistent ways which may be anticipated with some confidence across different times and places, but, understandable though it may be, to slip from this way of seeing their *activity* to describing them as such-and-such a kind of *person* is to rob them of their subjectivity and to deny them the possibility of self-initiated change.

A society in which what really counts more than anything else is what kind of an object one is, is almost inevitably going to end up paying particular attention to people as bodies. After all, objectivity values above all measurable physical dimensions, and even if we feel some slight discomfort about the plausibility of measuring 'personality', one thing that a person's body definitely does lend itself to is weighing and measuring; the body has the advantage of actually being an object in the physical world. Small wonder, then, that our culture is obsessed with physical appearance, and that some of the most acute and painful vulnerabilities that people experience are in connexion with their shape or size.

In recent years, of course, the feminist movement in particular has drawn angry attention to the ways in which women are exploited and abused as physical objects, and it is probably true that more women than men suffer tortures of shame and embarrassment, guilt and self-disgust over their bodies. Massive industries both fuel and feed on this sensitivity. Beauty is a possession which can be owned, or (more particularly) a commodity which can be bought. But it is not only women who suffer in this way, although they are more likely to feel unhappy about their bodies as a whole (that they are simply 'horrible' or 'disgusting' *in toto*); men frequently feel shame about particular parts of their body (noses, hair, genitals, hands, feet, etc.) or about their height (too short, too tall).

However much you may hide your ignoble thoughts or dissemble your baser feelings, your body can be instantly transfixed by the gaze of the Other, may become an all-enveloping emblem of shame from which there is no escape – or almost none. There is no chance of hiding your bulging stomach from your lover's eyes, and you await his judgment as a prisoner awaits the sentence from the bench. No judgment can be more cruel, no sentence harder to bear, than one about which the person can do nothing – even the prisoner can expiate his crime.

*Phyllis's husband — considered in most respects a kind, conscientious man — told her in a fit of spleen occasioned by her sexual unresponsiveness that he sometimes wished she looked like the girls on the Pirelli calendar at work – their breasts didn't look like fried eggs.*

Women – possibly because they are less enthusiastic objectifiers than men – seem less unthinkingly cruel in what they say to men, and, paradoxically perhaps (or simply because they are more used to it), seem quite often to receive such insults more stoically than most men would do.

*Geraldine talks quite cheerfully about her husband's opinion that her 'arse is like a jelly in a paper bag', and with only a flicker of pain in her eyes. She is in fact obsessed with her physical appearance, and has consulted cosmetic surgeons on more than one occasion, but sees this as her personal concern and is unaware of the potential judgment of the Other on which it rests.*

Not only may one be objectified by others into a particular bodily form, but as a paid-up member of the objectifying culture, may oneself use one's body as the objective peg on to which to hang a host of psychological difficulties: there are for example many women who would in any case by most current standards be accepted as looking unusually attractive but who themselves insist that their bodies are in some way substandard or 'horrible'. It is as if this, at least, would be a *tangible* difficulty, somehow easier to contemplate than the psychological complexities which in truth lie behind their anxiety. Even more paradoxically, unacceptable physical appearance may become a kind of protective shield behind which a person can shelter from the risk of engagement with the world. For example, obese people who try but fail to slim may sometimes be using what they see as their ugliness as an excuse for a dreaded lack of success in life or love: they can tell themselves that they are unsuccessful because they are fat, not because they are inept or unlovable, but to become slim in actuality would expose them to the risk of real failure. Thus although being, as it were, trapped in a body which does not come up to scratch in the eyes of the Other can be one of the most painful humiliations our culture can inflict on people, the defensive aims of objectivity may still be served, even to these people's advantage, by enabling them to use their physical shame to evade responsibility for what they do.

In the absence of a socially accepted and agreed sphere for the operation of subjectivity (which might render physical appearance irrelevant to issues of personal worth), people who find themselves trapped in negatively valued, objectified bodies have three main options. The first is simply to suffer the imposed labelling – ugliness, skinniness, fatness, etc. – possibly turning it to advantage in the way outlined in the previous paragraph. Such a stance is almost bound to be associated with enormous insecurity and rock-bottom self-esteem. The second is to make use of those services in our society which offer to put the problem right in its own terms, for example through body-building, cosmetic surgery, slimming courses, make-up, and so on. This course is by no means always easy, quite apart from the lack of reliability of many of the procedures involved, as it may conflict with other psychological needs: for example, obesity is often the result of comforting one's basic insecurity through eating, and in this case it becomes very difficult to slim and at the same time lose thereby the solace of food, so that insecurity, anxiety, shame and guilt (at periodically giving way to greed) all become compounded in one unhappy existence (in which, for example, binge eating followed by self-induced vomiting may play a prominent part, as may a kind of pervasive guilty secrecy and deceitfulness which extends into areas of life apparently quite unconnected with food).

*Because of her parents' – particularly her father's – brutality towards her, June was taken into care at the age of seven. At sixteen, she is a sweetly pretty, somewhat overweight girl who goes out of her way to charm those she meets with a kind of gentle pliability (towards women) and a mild sexual invitingness (towards men). And yet her inarticulate conception of herself is as rotten through and through. She overeats secretly and makes herself vomit, and the staff of the home she lives in have periodically to clear her room of hidden, half-eaten tins of putrefying food. She hoards dirty underwear in corners of cupboards and drawers until it becomes almost rancid, and she lies systematically about any aspect of her conduct (which in fact involves nearly all of it) which she thinks could put her in a bad light. Despite sometimes desperate efforts to make people love her, she is convinced that nobody could, so that sooner or later she rejects people who have grown fond of her before they get the chance to reject her. There is little in her life other than pain, veiled self-indulgence, secrecy, deceit and guilt. Her body she regards with loathing.*

Because their anxieties stem often from an unhappy but unexamined subjectivity, people who seek or permit the physical modification of their body through surgery (sometimes pursuing this aim with tremendous single-mindedness) may find once their efforts have been successful that the alteration to their objectified self leaves them no better off than before.

The third course open to those who find themselves imprisoned in a body they have come to hate is to demonstrate their indifference to it by attempting to overcome matter with spirit. In some ways this comes close to acknowledging the importance of subjectivity, but nevertheless still makes the mistake of overvaluing the body as an objectified symbol of self: the triumph consists not in acting upon the world *through* the body as an instrument of will, but in destroying or subjugating the body as a means of proving independence from it.

*After a miserable childhood, a disastrous marriage and a series of unhappy love affairs, Grace, who used to be a lively, attractive woman, and in many ways the social focus of her family and a wide circle of friends, suddenly became extremely 'phobic' (afraid under almost any circumstances to leave her home), withdrawn, and reticent about her feelings. It became a matter of honour with her not to disclose her unhappiness to anyone – even to her children to whom she was otherwise very close. She also found herself unable to eat proper cooked meals, and for years lived off tea and biscuits and the occasional sandwich. Naturally, she lost a great deal of weight, and became, physically, a shadow of her former self. To her great distress, she also found that at times, especially following some kind of emotional friction with someone important to her, she would experience a compulsion to lacerate her body (usually parts of her limbs not exposed to public view) with a piece of broken glass which she kept especially for this purpose. She began to accept only after a long time in psychotherapy that her experiences and activities – which before she had found frightening and alien – could be made sense of as an attempt to establish the independence of her spirit and her will from bodily needs and the need for affection from others. It is of course by no means certain that this is a correct interpretation, but it certainly helped, for both Grace and her therapist, to clarify an otherwise extremely puzzling set of circumstances.*

There are many people who display a kind of self-denying asceticism towards their bodily needs, as if any self-indulgence would swamp them with a kind of obliterating objectivity from which there would be no escape: they are aware that the objectified body is a trap, and yet are trapped in their very hostility towards it, cut off from any way of conceptualizing their subjectivity other than as a battle against the flesh, and quite unable to enjoy themselves. Several psychologists and psychiatrists have suggested that this kind of fundamental attitude may be what lies behind the puzzling phenomenon named officially 'anorexia nervosa'. Perhaps one of the most illuminating accounts of this condition is, however, not that of an 'expert', but has been written by someone who herself suffered very acutely from it.*

---

*See Sheila MacLeod, *The Art of Starvation*, Virago Press, 1981.

The fact that (particularly female) beauty is regarded as a *possession* in our culture, means that those who do not meet the quite narrow standards established for it, or 'lose' it through the normal processes of ageing, etc., experience a great deal of shame and pain which might be avoided if (as I shall argue in a later chapter could usefully be encouraged) its fundamentally subjective character were more widely acknowledged. It may, in other words, be much more the case that beauty is truly in the eye of the beholder, a phenomenon of personal relationship, rather than an attribute to be measured by the impersonal gaze of the Other.

The insistence of our culture on turning people into objectified selves, collections of measurable characteristics centred in bodies valued almost solely for their appearance, means that some form of *self-consciousness* is virtually inescapable. A child may just manage to exist for a few years in an unself-conscious absorption with a world to which it relates through its more or less unreflecting activity, but it cannot survive for long without becoming aware of the importance of others' opinions of it as an object, and so it must learn to dissemble its feelings, attend to its appearance, conform to official standards of education and attainment, manipulate its image so that its status relative to others can be maximized. This requires a constant monitoring of how the self appears to others, an unremitting concern with 'impression management' and a developing expertise in understanding and handling the conceptual apparatus and values of objectivity – the ingestion and acceptance, that is, of the standards of our mythifying culture. 'What does the Other think of me?' becomes the single most important question which can be asked.

Success at the game of impression management entails an almost wilful overlooking of the experience of social life rendered by the kind of intuitive sensitivity discussed towards the beginning of this chapter. Although, certainly, one could not operate fluently in the world without *tacitly* making use of such sensitivity, it is perfectly possible *explicitly* to disavow or disown it. Everyone in one sense knows that the emperor is naked (just as, for example, everyone knows that possession of a Rolls Royce and a beautiful wife is totally irrelevant to an individual's personal worth) but it is expedient to deny what one sees and to profess one's faith in the prevailing values – and if you play your cards right you might end up with the Rolls Royce and the wife, and, most important of all, the admiration from the Other which goes with them. If, on the other hand, you insist on your knowledge of the emperor's nakedness, you may not find the ready assent from others which could confidently be expected only if you assume their good faith toward their own experience; in fact, their strenuous denial that they share your experience may leave you in such isolation that ultimately not only they but you yourself begin to question your sanity.

It is, I think, precisely the stance one takes towards experience rendered by intuitive sensitivity which determines the kind of self-consciousness one will develop (bearing in mind that, as things are, self-consciousness is inescapable).

Those people who are considered psychologically 'healthy' in our society are on the whole those who have a confident appreciation of themselves as satisfactory objects; they have learned, that is, successfully to manage the impression they give to others, and to extort from them a validation of how they wish to appear. They have also learned that to preserve the relative comfort offered by this mode of existence they must disregard or deny what their intuition tells them about its falsity (persuade themselves that the emperor is not really naked); they have describable 'selves' which can, in the best objective tradition, be broken down into a series of positively valued traits or attributes. The truth, of course, is that human existence is uncertain and vulnerable, complex and delicate, and human relationships shot through with pain and threat as well as joy and comfort. The evidence for this truth is available to all but the wilfully blind. The advantage of wilful blindness (of allegiance, that is, to the coarsened values of objectivity) is that it obviates the necessity for the kind of gentle, sensitive, risky, tentative, dangerous transactions required for the conduct of civilized, caring relationships; it replaces the agonizing difficulties raised by questions to do with the morality of our conduct towards one another with the simplified values of the market economy. It is thus in the interests of the socially 'successful' to treat people as things or commodities, and to disregard those aspects of their own experience which suggest that to do so is a distortion of the truth.

There are, however, also those who are unable to escape the evidence of their intuitive sensitivity, even although, often, they can well appreciate the expediency of doing so. Many people who find themselves unable to disregard the insights they gain into the motives and feelings of those around them see their sensitivity as a kind of affliction. I remember one patient who talked for a long time about her 'weakness' until I realized that what she meant was an unusually accurate sensitivity to the real feelings of the members of her family, and in particular to the petty dishonesties and tactical subterfuges to which they resorted in their dealings with each other. Her father in particular had spent most of his time during her childhood in trying to bully her out of her perceptions (even to the extent of threatening physical torture if she did not deny what she knew to be true). She felt confused and guilty about her empathetic ability to understand others, seeing herself as if cursed with the possession of a kind of original sin which made her unworthy of their company. And yet she could not abandon her sensitivity, despite the fact that most of the rest of the population seemed to find it easy to do so.

The affliction of intuitive sensitivity is experienced most often in the form of shyness – the form, that is, of self-consciousness negatively valued in our culture. Not all kinds of shyness stem from this origin, but it does seem to be the case that many of those who experience shyness to an excruciating degree are at the same time people who are very acutely aware of the emotional currents passing between themselves and others. Very shy people often have a kind of raw, flinching sensitivity to others, so that they approach them like cats testing the bounds of their territory. The shy person's consciousness of self is nothing like that of the confident impression manager: the shy person is aware only of a painfully inadequate, useless, negatively valued self, or even of a complete lack of self ('I've got no personality'). In this respect, perhaps, shy people are close to the recognition of a truth which their more confident fellows have more successfully repressed, i.e. that in fact selves of the kind of which they so painfully feel the lack are mythical inventions of an objectifying culture. But they are not on the whole able to articulate this truth nor to gain any comfort from it; instead, they are to be found standing in corners, aching with a sense of their own futility and uninterestingness to others, searching despairingly and vainly for the words that will introduce them to others as worthy of attention and acknowledgment, enviously wondering at the apparent smoothness and ease with which others seem to fill out their existence as forces to be reckoned with and confidently conduct their relations with each other. At the same time, the shy person may secretly harbour a kind of arrogant contempt for the shallowness and boringness of the easy socializer he or she so bitterly envies, finding solace in the view that when social contacts do materialize in his or her world, they have at least got real depth and significance. But the all too familiar experience is for two shy people, at a party for example, to end up together in a corner, each embarrassed at the obviousness to the others around them of their pathetically settling for safety in mutual support, each secretly disgusted that they could not appeal to someone less like themselves. It is hard to escape the objective culture, and thus not to experience shyness as a crippling affliction. Wherever he or she goes, the shy person feels positively magnified under the gaze of the Other, the inadequacies of self exposed even to the most fleeting glance and most casual encounter, and yet quite unable to abandon his or her intuitive sensitivity to social relations in order to join in the game of impression management.

Although unable successfully to manipulate their appearance as objects, and although the values implicit in their sensitivity have much more to do with subjectivity than objectivity, shy people's experience of themselves is often as almost completely objectified: only others, it seems, can act freely and control their own fate, only others can have opinions or attitudes or feelings which could make an impact on someone's life. For shy people the Other is everywhere, and it never occurs to them that they could be Other for others, that anyone could care what *they* thought about things. They are paralysed, others are free.

That some people seem so easily to be able to disregard their own experience in favour of an objectifying mythology while others are tormented by their inability to do anything other than take their experience seriously presents us with a mystery for which there seems to be no satisfactory explanation, particularly in view of the fact that, as I have suggested, intuitive sensitivity is often maintained despite a wish that it should not be, and in the face of constant discouragement from others that it should be. The kind of shyness which is experienced as so distressing that it drives a person to seek professional help for it seems often to stem from a particular set of circumstances (though this need by no means always be the case). The most familiar pattern is where people found themselves alone as sensitive children in relatively insensitive families, receiving no particular support from anybody for their somewhat inward (but probably psychologically quite accurate) view of things.

Never confirmed as an objective self in the same way as those around them (indeed, quite often strenuously disconfirmed as such) they end up with a strong sense of personal worthlessness but an equally strong conviction that their personal experience yields insights about people and their relations with each other which cannot be discounted. Nearly all those who complain in later life of experiencing anxiety so great that it disrupts their lives describe themselves as having been shy as children. It is thus generally felt in our culture that shyness is a negative characteristic, to be discouraged where possible in children, and treated if necessary in adults.

However, it seems to me that this is so only because of the coarsely insentitive values of objectivity to which most of us bear allegiance. Because, perhaps, of their greater awareness of the complexity, delicacy and danger inherent in our relations with each other, shy people often (though again, of course, not always) treat others more kindly and gently, more empathetically and conscientiously than their more confident fellows, and may show greater psychological honesty and perceptiveness than is possible if one is to be successful in the brashly competitive world of objectivity.

Shy people are not always wrong to fear the hostility and ridicule of others, since, though painfully and against their will, they may represent a living challenge to objective values, a threat to the continued maintenance of myth. It is perhaps particularly in young male society that the shy person runs the greatest risk of teasing and humiliation, because it is precisely here that objectifying insensitivity is maintained with greatest tenacity. Broadly speaking, young men tend more than anyone else to repudiate their tenderness and vulnerability, and a shy person in their midst threatens to draw their attention to sensitivities they would rather ignore. For a shy young man there can be almost no experience more excruciating than suffering daily the hostile banter of his fellows in a workshop, office or factory, and the degree of isolation and self-doubt that can be generated in such situations, in the absence of solid confirmation or support, can be almost if not quite unhingeing.

Whether virtue or vice, social disease or (as I have tended to argue here) potential spiritual strength, shyness is certainly not comfortable, and does not make for a rewarding life. The obvious answer to this is of course to seek methods of 'treating' shyness in order either to mitigate its more painful effects or to transform it into the kind of confidence which the shy person

longs for and envies so much in others. This answer is, however, only obvious if the basic values of our culture remain unquestioned. If, indeed, one were to imagine a world populated
entirely by the kinds of people we tend in general to regard as
most successful and 'adjusted' – for example by the kinds of
'stars' and 'personalities' whose lives are thought so worthy of
our attention by gossip columnists and television producers –
one might quickly find onself longing for the presence of a little
pained sensitivity and inarticulate, tongue-tying feeling in
those around us, for without it we should stand in danger of
being overwhelmed by the artificial and the fake. Only sensitivity
to our own experience can drag us back from self-deception.

There is nothing objectively 'wrong' with shy people, it is
simply that they are misplaced in a culture which cannot afford
to endorse their experience. It would seem in the long run more
valuable to question the standards of the culture than to
attempt to change the people.

One does of course come across a fortunate, but extremely
small minority of people who manage to conduct themselves
sensitively and spontaneously in the world without recourse to
fake objectified selves and without suffering the tortures of
shyness; people, that is, who are confident in their subjectivity,
guided by their own experience (their intuitive sensitivity), and
yet able to relate warmly and openly to others without feeling
threatened and without having to take refuge in some specialized creed or dogma to protect them from the Other's objectifying gaze. But the very rarity of such people must lead us to
question the healthiness of our social and psychological climate
in which the vast majority can survive only by succumbing to
the prevailing mythifying standards or by aligning themselves
with an opposition to those standards which convinces itself of
its worth through adherence to, for example, freakish religious
dogmas or a kind of uniform, organized anarchy (itself often
orchestrated and exploited by the very forces it purports to
challenge).

Most people, then, have given subjectivity up as a bad job.

The prevalence and force of objectivity creates conditions
which make it very hard for people to exist as individual subjects, relatively easy for them to experience themselves and
others as objects. We have dissociated ourselves from our subjectivity (which, however, we cannot totally eradicate, and
which runs riot behind the scenes, creating the myths which we
take as the objective standards which must rule our lives) and

can therefore only experience life passively, as objects. As people, therefore, we are morally paralysed and powerless – rather than being responsible for our own conduct, we see our 'behaviour' as at the mercy of blind natural laws, the existence of which we may establish through the objective methods given us by 'science', but which we cannot conceive as being created by ourselves. Indeed, it has always been one of the more euphoric claims of those bewitched by the determinist and mechanist dogmas of 'modern science' that morality itself is defunct as a conception necessary to the understanding of man's 'behaviour', and is relevant only to the blurred and murky intellectual scene which preceded the scientific enlightenment. The fallacy of such reasoning is, I should have thought, blindingly obvious (since our subjectivity is so clearly at work in the rejection of our subjectivity!) but its influence nevertheless pervades our lives at every turn.

Having the status of object, certainly, may promise (as it happens, I think, falsely) to release us from some of the terrors attendant on subjectivity – for example, from some forms of psychological pain, loneliness and responsibility, fragility and the threat of fundamental failure, the necessity for individual courage and decisiveness. Objective status also delivers, when it is working well, a certain kind of passive material comfort, an apparent freedom from effort in our daily lives and in the conduct of our relations with each other. The lot of the table tennis ball may not be an entirely happy one, but it is spared the tensions experienced by the players, the painful necessity for training and practice, the threat of humiliating defeat – at all times it is neutral with respect to the 'rules' which actually govern its behaviour (which are of course enacted by the players) and could, if endowed with a modicum of reflective consciousness, comfort itself with the thought that there is in any case nothing it could do to improve its situation. By placing ourselves in a universe in which *we* are subject to the interplay of laws objectively established as independent of us, we create conditions for ourselves very similar to those of the table tennis ball – batted to and fro, often painfully perhaps, but at least without having to take the responsibility for it.

This, indeed, is how many people seem to experience their lives – so used to responding passively to the force of circumstances that when called upon for some kind of stance, some kind of directing, subjective moral initiative of their own, they are left limp and confused, searching helplessly for a directive from somewhere else, for the requisite objective solution to release them from their dilemma. This is particularly evident, for example, in the sphere of child upbringing. Since we have forgotten that children are subjective, and therefore moral beings, we expect them to develop like objects manufactured in stages or, nurtured only by the provision of material necessities, like plants or vegetables which can be relied upon to produce the desired characteristics at the appropriate time. As far as giving *direction* to their children is concerned, many people seem to feel that this is none of their business, and can only be done by reference to the appropriate experts and authorities, since how people *ought* to be is, like everything else, a matter to be established and programmed objectively. Thus grown men and women will expect their children to achieve that same estate without any moral guidance or example from them – satisfactory upbringing in this sense will, it is expected, be achieved through the school, the experts, the television, material indulgence, etc., no matter what the extent of parental neglect of or indifference to their children's spiritual development, and independently of whatever kind of example of how people are (and should be) the parents themselves knowingly or unknowingly set.

It is perhaps a sign of the very times I am criticizing that I am likely to be misunderstood as suggesting here that children should be more severely disciplined and strictly trained in the conventional moralities than they are. But in using the word 'moral' I do not mean to be moralistic, but to point rather to the necessity for taking a deliberate stance (as opposed to occupying one unwittingly and accidentally) towards questions of how we should conduct ourselves with each other, of taking an interest in and being concerned with the way a person develops, recognizing and trying to meet their spiritual and emotional needs, making room for them to develop their special interests and abilities, advocating those standards which seem truly in the person's best interests and have been confirmed in the parents' own experience, and so on. For the objectified individual, all such questions (and they are, of course, certainly not unproblematic!) are fraught with threat and difficulty, so that the easiest choice in bringing up children is either to oppress them or indulge them and leave the process of 'socialization' to those (mythically) better trained to deal with them. The end result, naturally enough, is a generation of hostile or bemused adolescents who have even less conception of themselves as subjective people, as moral beings, than the parents who presided so helplessly and non-committally over their development.

To *stand for* something, whether in child-rearing or any other sphere, is of course to risk error; it is also to challenge one's status as object and to become conspicuous under the gaze of the Other, to give away one's position and to invite rejection. But it is also the only way through which social evolution can take a truly moral direction; it is the inescapable consequence of recognizing and taking seriously the fact that it is *we* who make the world, not 'it' or 'them'.

In the prevailing conditions it is of course quite likely that anyone who does take a stance will stand out as eccentric in some way, or will certainly feel in danger of so doing; in any case he or she is likely to find it a lonely experience.

*Annett (p.25) is one of those people who have been unable to abandon their own experience. She observes others with an acute intuitive sensitivity which she communicates with great warmth and humour, and her descriptions of what passes between herself and those she is close to strike me often as highly perceptive. She can at times be movingly passionate about what she sees as valuable or suspect about the way people treat each other, and takes, for example, a deep interest in her own and others' children, so that she might find herself reflecting for hours at a time on the significance for her of a relatively fleeting (and by others unnoticed) event. Though she had a less than average education and comes from what most would consider a rather deprived background, there would clearly, were she given the chance, be few intellectual tasks beyond her. But despite all this she experiences herself as a kind of ludicrous simpleton, feeling that people regard her as a mildly contemptible oddity, impractical and unable to deal sensibly and stably with the ordinary demands of life. Partly, certainly, she is blind to the degree to which people do in fact appreciate her, but partly also she is an isolated moral force in a sea of objects who see her propensity for taking stands as mere foolhardiness.*

Our culture seems to have much to offer those who opt for an objective existence: libraries and popular bookshops, for example, are full of advice on what objective rules to follow to bring about a wide range of desired end results, from becoming slim and beautiful to achieving sexual joy, phenomenal powers of memory, ability as a creative writer, successful motherhood, and so on. You simply practice the 'skills' which the experts have managed to distil from their objective knowledge of things. But there is very little on offer *at the same level of availability* to those who seek help in enlarging their understanding of what their own experience tells them to be the case, in elaborating and enriching the stand they feel bound to take – indeed, they might well find themselves admonished for their temerity and advised to leave any such dangerously subjective enterprise to those better qualified to understand such things. Thus whoever takes a stand does so in fear and trembling, and no doubt their risk of error is greater because of their isolation from any confirming culture which acknowledges the value of subjectivity. Moral support is in short supply.

Drained of subjectivity, we are deprived of all those potentialities which are associated with it – instead of acting we can only react, we can consume but not create, follow but not initiate, conform but not determine. Objectivity devalues and ultimately nullifies the abstract, the spiritual and the moral, replacing them with a coarse materialism which brutally asserts its own justification as simply self-evident. Nothing which is not concrete and measurable is held to exist – ideas, meanings, emotions, wishes, intentions, are dismissed as pre-behaviourist, 'mentalistic' clap-trap. Thus the person finds him- or herself as a mechanism in a machine world, confused, helpless and morally paralysed because out of touch with any means of influencing that world, frightened and bewildered when personal experience suggests that the myths of objectivity do not in fact confer the blessings expected of them, but still unable to harness that semi-articulate experience to any effective form of intervention as the world becomes more and more dehumanized.

Security and passive stimulation through consumption have become our primary preoccupations. To escape the annihilating possibility of an entirely negative objectification and to enjoy the material 'benefits' of a mechanized existence constitute, respectively, our greatest anxiety and our foremost aim. The operation of these concerns is clearly to be seen even in what ought otherwise to be our most delicate and tender transactions: for example, sexual love becomes in part a battle to hide and protect one's most vulnerable, tender sensitivities from the partner at the same time as extorting from him or her the maximum of physical stimulation. Not seeing that tenderness and sexuality are inextricably related, and that denial of the former leads to impoverishment of the latter, the objectified 'lover' is seized by a craving for stimulation which becomes the more desperate in proportion to the emotional anaesthesia which underlies it – an anaesthesia which is likely to be mis-identified as arising from, perhaps, a lack of 'expertise', or an unduly prudish attitude to what, it is thought, ought to be the limitless opportunities of sexual licence, in which pornography, mechanical aids, 'sex therapy' and so on all have their proper part to play. Only someone prepared to abandon his or her subjective experience in favour of an objectifying, mechanizing mythology would find him- or herself supporting this kind of sexual philosophy; the solemn reverence in which sex therapy is held by professional psychologists and psychiatrists, as well as the enormous economic success of the sex-aid and porno-graphy 'industries', suggest that such abandonment of experi-ence is on no small scale.

Many people who seek help for sexual 'problems' view them-selves in this way – with, that is, a kind of bemused objectivity which utterly fails to place their sexuality in the context of a relationship (although 'relationship' is a word all too glibly used to characterize the unexamined situation in which two nervous or hostile strangers find themselves in bed together). Sex has become a mechanized commodity (in which failure of the sexual 'equipment' is seen precisely as mechanical breakdown), and the pursuit of sexual satisfaction a feverish campaign which, because it misperceives the nature of intimacy, is doomed to empty frustration. Sex is, indeed, our sad substitute for in-timacy: the last shred of comfort which can be extracted by some of those (frequently women) most damaged and objecti-fied by our depersonalizing culture is through their being physically arousing to another.

*Apart from a somewhat coldly critical concern that she should conform to conventional standards of behaviour, Mar-garet's mother had been largely indifferent to her as a child, leaving the practical aspects of her upbringing to an older sister, who herself had taken on the job none too willingly. Her step-father, on the other hand, was viciously punitive towards her, and was particularly suspicious and censorious about possible sexual misdemeanours, even before she had reached puberty. Margaret's primary conception of herself is as an obstacle, a nuisance, a bad object, there only to inconvenience the lives of*

*others. She is shy, slightly awkward and ungainly in her move-*
*ments, and has an underfed, pinched air about her. Her clothes*
*have a distinctly second-hand look, suited more to a maiden*
*aunt than a girl of nineteen. She has no friends of either sex.*
*Surprisingly, in view of a rather incongruous primness and*
*conventionality about her manner, she confesses with anguish*
*that she considers herself morally beyond the pale, as she is*
*virtually addicted to a disco club in town, following attendance*
*at which she almost invariably finds herself having sex with*
*someone on the building site which adjoins it. The boys or men*
*are never the same, and they never take her home or ask her out.*
*Following these episodes she always feels shame and disgust*
*with herself, and vows never to go back. A lot of things in her*
*experience of her past life seem to contribute to this almost*
*compulsive pattern, but not the least important factor is that*
*these brief, sad and in many ways degrading sexual encounters*
*provide the only warmth in her existence: even she can stimulate*
*someone else's body to some kind of interest in her, and be*
*wanted for a moment. It is important to note that Margaret feels*
*no sexual satisfaction or excitement in these 'relationships', and*
*indeed in this respect feels positively anaesthetized.*

Freud did us no great service, perhaps, in suggesting that
the origin of intimacy and tenderness is to be found in sexuality, but this view still holds sway despite the arguments
which have been levelled against it, forcefully and cogently, by
several influential psychologists and psychiatrists since Freud's
time.* Only the adult who has overlooked what it was like to be
exposed to the full blast of what H. S. Sullivan called the 'lust
dynamism' could mistake the child's need for and expression of
tenderness as 'really' sexual, and Freud's views have always
stretched the credulity of those who have paid serious attention
to their own and others' experience of sexuality as it makes
itself known in puberty. This is not, of course, to say that
non-sexual love and tenderness do not entail their own powerful and potentially destructive forces, nor that hatred and
jealousy form no part of the child's experience. The appeal of
Freud's view can in part be understood in the opportunities it
presents for objectifying the otherwise subjective, and in some
respects abstract concept (faculty, experience) of love. Though

* See, for example, I. D. Suttie, *The Origins of Love and Hate*, Penguin Books,
1960; H. S. Sullivan, *The Interpersonal Theory of Psychiatry*, Tavistock
Publications, 1953; E. Fromm, *The Art of Loving*, Allen & Unwin, 1957.

only indirectly a concern of Freud's, the possibilities for measurement and reduction to physical properties offered by the identification of love with sex were too good to be missed, and an uncomfortably subjective phenomenon was turned into a manageably objective one. Freud thus played into the hands of a concern for objectification already rampant in our culture, the subsequent achievements of which are readily to be seen all around us. These include the belief (which of course engenders the appropriate 'behaviour') that a 'good' sex life will provide the foundation of happiness and satisfactory relationships, as well as the confused response to the discovery that this does not actually happen. In fact, sex out of the context of an intimate and loving relationship is not usually found to be particularly satisfying at all, but because of the power of the myth of the primary importance of sex, experience of this is attended most often by an increasingly desperate attempt to extort validity for the mythical proposition. In this way an anaesthetized sexuality has to be increasingly stimulated and heated up if it is to be preserved at all in its mythified role as the foundation of our psychological structure and the origin of our possibilities of relationship.

The fact that we must relate to each other as objects, the continuous presence of the Other's gaze which threatens almost literally to turn us to stone, mean that real intimacy is indeed almost impossible to achieve. Intimacy would involve an effort to explore each other's subjectivity, to listen charitably and experience empathetically, to shun labels and categories, to be alert to uniqueness, to allow the possibility of evolution in the psychological and relational spheres, to acknowledge uncertainty and creativity while trying to articulate and examine in good faith the stance we take to each other and the world. Instead, the characteristic and familiar way we relate to one another in our objectified interpersonal space is to bristle with suspicion and hostility as we seek to evade and impose our labels on each other. We listen to each other only with ears cocked critically for objective fallacies in argument, itching to anchor the struggle for meaning in some concretely measurable error. Most conversations between two people are double monologues in which each party seeks to establish for him- or herself a kind of massively impregnable solidity of 'being'. We project our safely established objective evaluations over each other, anxiously attempting to expunge every trace of ambiguity or uncertainty, only satisfied when we have pinned down and categorized each other like so many dead butterflies, suitably varnished with the viscous language we have developed to prevent the last possibility of change.

# 4   The Domination of Words

Without the use of language we should not be able to represent either to each other or to ourselves our views of reality and truth. It is only through using words that we can agree about the nature of the world and describe our experience, make objective what we sense and feel, give concrete form to dimly perceived meanings, build concepts which we may test against the experience of others, extend our processes of thought and memory so that we can criticize and elaborate them to a degree of complexity which would otherwise be quite impossible. We live in a medium of words.

In giving concrete, objective form to our experience, words take on a kind of hard finality which makes them difficult to resist as the determiners of truth. *Sharing* the meanings of words constitutes an important step towards objectifying the things they refer to – clearly, nothing could be considered objectively established if individuals could not be brought to agree about its nature. In this way language implies almost by necessity an objective world, since, if its members are to be able to communicate sensibly, the community which speaks a given language *must* share the meanings embodied in it. This object in my hand is a pencil, and about that one would expect every competent speaker of English to agree: it is 'true' that it is a pencil, a 'real' object in the world, about the existence and nature of which it is easy to suppose there can be no dispute. Naming something goes a long way towards defining it objec- tively, and we can quite easily forget that the name is in fact no more than a conventional sign for a whole complex of mean- ings, experiences, expectations, etc. Through language the un- known is made known, the inarticulate articulated. Simply to describe something is to remove from it a degree of anxiety- arousing mystery. Patients told their diagnosis may feel re- lieved even though they have not the slightest idea what the diagnosis signifies. Popular science programmes on the tele- vision thrive merely through giving names and incomprehensible descriptions to phenomena utterly mysterious to the viewer. ('This', says the presenter, 'is a molecule' – and the camera zooms in on a structure of wire and plastic balls, leaving the average viewer not already acquainted with molecules presum- ably satisfied but surely none the wiser.)

Of course, it is obvious on reflection that words are in a sense arbitrary, that, even when their meanings are universally shared, they carry no reality in themselves, no guarantee of objective truth (where 'objective' here implies a truth beyond what people simply agree about). A pencil could equally well be called something else, and in any case lays claim to our attention only because we have endowed it with a particular function: it cannot be considered apart from the human purposes we have created it for. Even a pencil is not exactly a 'thing in itself'. But though this is fairly obvious, I think that in the ordinary course of our daily lives we forget that words are things which, fundamentally, are attached to our experience for reasons which suit us. Even logical truths (like $2+2=4$) are presumably of interest only to human minds. But rather than seeing words as our own creation, we become mesmerized by them and by the concepts which we have created with them, and we find it hard to shake off the idea that they relate to an absolute and *impersonal* reality. We tend to forget that words are the result of our imperfect struggle to articulate our experience (and thereby to *create* an elaborate linguistic network of metaphor for our experience), and see them instead as the representatives of a reality which *imposes itself upon* us objectively.

In many matters of general agreement – as, for example, what constitutes a pencil – doubts and difficulties about truth and reality can for present purposes be left to philosophers. In other areas, however, this is not the case. For example, there are many areas of discourse in which the ordinary person takes on trust the 'fact' that names are meaningful in the same way that 'pencil' seems to be meaningful. This is particularly the case where names carry the endorsement of experts – especially 'scientific' experts. Few people not acquainted with psychiatric controversy, for example, would question that there is a 'mental disease' called 'schizophrenia'. Yet many people who are so acquainted argue that the concept of 'mental disease' is a myth (which may perhaps be another way of saying that, on closer acquaintance with the phenomena involved, it is *not* the case that, for example, 'schizophrenia' refers to anything about which agreement is possible in the way that 'pencil' does). I believe that much of the language we use to describe our psychological distress and the social context in which it occurs is mythical in this sense. Our everyday language, thus, supports the mythical view of the world discussed in Chapter 1, and many of the verbal concepts we use are those imposed upon us by our cultural bias towards objectivity.

It might be objected here that if, as I have suggested, words are attached to experience arbitrarily, then *any* verbal formulation of experience is mythical. But by 'arbitrary' what I mean to suggest is that words in themselves have no *necessary* reality or guarantee of accuracy, even though they appear to single something out in experience to make it real. I do not mean to say that words become attached to our experience haphazardly or at random. *How* we attach words to experience will reflect the purposes for which we wish to use them: for example, either to try to describe our experience as accurately as possible, or, on the other hand, to force it into pre-set moulds.

These points will perhaps seem obvious to anyone who has given any thought to such matters, but it may nevertheless be worth reminding those (both lay and professional) who too readily take it on trust that the nature of the world as described by prestigious and socially accredited people (doctors, scientists, academics, psychologists) must be accurate, that such is by no means necessarily the case. Indeed, there seems to me to be a real danger that, at the everyday level of social living, we may become unaware of there being any reality beyond language: what can be *said*, if it is uttered with enough authority, or by someone with a sufficiently convincing 'image', simply becomes part of the received truth and does not have to be questioned or judged. Evaluation and judgment are subjective faculties which pay attention to the content of an utterance and decide whether or not to accept it. Passive acquiescence, on the other hand, is manipulated by 'authorized' sources of objectivity, in which the content of the utterance is unimportant compared to the 'credibility' of the utterer (hence, presumably, the obsessive concern of the news media with 'images' and 'personalities' as against the actual substance of what people say). We have, in other words, given up our ability to judge the nature of the world, to believe or disbelieve in any *active* sense, but rather wait in a slightly bemused way for our opinions to be revealed to us by those accredited to do so. 'Belief', indeed, is a concept anathema to objectivity, because it is rooted in the subjective person rather than in the 'verifiable', concrete structures of the world; so, in our objectifying language, the *activity* of believing is turned into the *possession* of 'credibility'. That the Other has credibility removes from you the trouble of believing or disbelieving. Words are the medium through which we become turned into passively consuming objects; they cut us off from access to our own judgment and experience because they impose upon us a ready-made world which we must accept as true because it is objective.

If this state of affairs is to be counteracted, it becomes vital to reassert the distinction between experience and language. This is not necessarily an easy distinction to make, since experience and language are so clearly interrelated, and indeed without language the distinction could not be made at all, nor could experience be described. It is also possible to argue that language *determines* the form of our experience, so that the two could not be considered as in any sense distinct. It is certainly true that one could not *think*, in the sense in which that term is usually taken, nor reflect upon experience, without the use of words. It is also true, however, that words are *not* necessary for the execution of highly complex and purposeful activity which must depend for its success to a great extent on the organized living-out of experience (there are many different ways of trying to say this, none of them very satisfactory: for example, one might say that we live out our experience in an organized manner, or that we act in an experienced manner, or that we have ways of organizing our experience which are not verbal). Anybody who doubts the phenomenon I am trying to refer to need only watch a cat catching a mouse.

These issues do not allow simple answers, and are, clearly, philosophically and psychologically very complex. However, quite apart from the academic arguments involved, my own experience of, in particular, collaborating with patients in the investigation of their difficulties and dilemmas convinces me that it is important to focus on the distinction between experience and language, and that doing so reveals two very clear functions of language which are not immediately apparent to naive reflection. The first, already touched upon, is that language has come to be used in our society as, so to speak, the blunt instrument of objectivity; the second is that, in this age at least, the primary function of language has become that of misrepresenting the truth.

The world is given to us in our experience. Indeed, as infants, we experience the world in advance of any ability to describe it, and we make our most fundamental evaluations of and distinctions between our experiences long before we have acquired language (it has always seemed to me entirely wrong to assume that babies are somehow not very clever: the intellectual demands on a new-born infant must be enormous, and its ability to deal with them prodigious).

The use of language gives us two possibilities in relation to our experience: we can describe it (to others, or, more essentially, to ourselves) either in good faith or in bad faith. We can, that is, either use the linguistic tools that become available to us to represent as accurately as possible the nature of the world we find in our experience, or we can attempt to force our experience into the ready-made (objective) structures which are culturally embedded in our language. To take the first course is to remain true to our intuitive sensitivity, to take the second is to run the risk of succumbing to the prevailing mythology.

Language presents us with the opportunity for constructing realities alternative to that given more immediately in our experience. The opportunities open to animals to misrepresent the nature of the projects they engage in are not great, though they are certainly not absent. A dog admonished as it starts to enact a clear intention to steal the Sunday joint may feign a kind of indifference to the meat, perhaps by diverting its stealthy approach to some more innocent aim; gestures of sub mission nullify what was but a moment before a cat's blatantly aggressive conduct. But on the whole such attempts at dissembling are transparent and easily understood, and there is little chance of an animal being able to lie effectively in the sense, for example, of pursuing a project while appearing not to (unless its entire existence is an embodied deception, as through the medium of camouflage). But human beings may much more easily pursue a particular line of conduct while using the possibilities given by language to claim that their intentions are quite otherwise.

*Ben's mother told him one day: 'You have two ways of smiling – one when you're happy, and one when you've been naughty.' The following day she walked into the kitchen when Ben (aged three) was taking some forbidden sweets from a cupboard. He turned towards her, smiling, and said: 'I'm smiling because I'm happy.'*

Quite apart from the chances it gives us for lying and dissembling, the magic of language enables a palliative gloss to be placed over painful experience, and the power of words is such that, once a person has become linguistically accomplished, an alternative construction of experience can be as compelling as the experience itself. Since the means whereby we represent experience to ourselves are linguistic (i.e., we can only *think* about experience through the use of words) we become in some senses the victims of our own articulateness; it can come to seem that what we tell ourselves is all there is to tell, that reality *is* what we tell ourselves about it. And further, language already contains culturally constructed palliatives for painful or puzzling experience – the child may find it hard to question its mother's authoritative view that, for example, its rage or frustration is 'tiredness', which is but a small step from accepting, say, the doctor's view that terror-stricken confusion is 'schizophrenia'. Our ability to reflect upon our experience is only as good as the linguistic tools available to us to do so – the less articulate person may have an awareness that 'something is not quite right', but will not be able to make that awareness concrete without having his or her consciousness 'raised' through the provision of finer and more sensitive (linguistic) concepts. (This is one of the ways in which the more educated exercise dominion over the lesser.) For everyday purposes, it seems that reality *is* the best description I am able to give myself of it.

One need only reflect on one's own experience to be convinced of the power language has to construct alternative versions of events – think, for example, of an occasion when something happened between you and somebody else which constituted at the time a painful blow to your pride or an enraging threat to your peace of mind. The chances are that in the course of the hours following this event you reconstructed it 'in your mind' several times (i.e. told yourself several alternative explanatory versions of it) until you settled on a version which seemed best to account for the facts. The chances are, too, that the version which best accounted for the facts was also one which left least injury to your self-esteem.

The relativity of 'truth' is nowhere more evident than in the accounts married couples give of issues of contention between them. It is a familiar experience for 'marital therapists' to find that, as they make their assessment during the initial stages of therapy, they are so impressed by the wife's account of her husband's brutality and insensitivity – so coherent, heart-felt and well integrated is her story – that they can scarcely contain their indignation. When the husband is interviewed, however, *his* account of the same events shifts them into a new perspective, in which his pained reasonableness, his desperate frustration at his wife's capriciousness, can only testify, so it seems, to the truth of what he is saying. One does not, of course, conclude that either partner is lying – both stories are in one perfectly good sense 'true', but both are indeed stories – accounts that each party has elaborated to him- or herself until they accord most comfortably with the reality each has constructed. Where one's self-esteem is implicated, it is extremely hard to stand in a relation of good faith to one's own experience.

One of the myths most firmly embedded in our popular culture is that the individual has a special claim to accuracy when accounting for his or her own conduct – that I can see better than you what my projects and motives are. Thus it is not on the whole considered inappropriate, when seeking an explanation for someone's conduct, to ask him why he did it – indeed, there are many situations in which it is considered not only proper but essential to extract such an account, as if its extraction provided the shortest and most accurate route to the truth. This is not to say, however, that, for example, the indignant parent or the suspicious policeman does not recognize that the person subject to inquiry might lie about his motives, but it does suggest that there is an expectation that the truth is available to him if he chooses to tell it.

However, anybody used to talking to small children who have not yet achieved a practised ability to give plausible accounts of their actions will have been struck frequently by the nature of their inability to render any such account. The question 'why did you do it?', however insistently posed, is likely to be met by a kind of blank puzzlement which only those blunted by insensitivity or blinded by theoretical prejudice are likely to interpret as just a stubborn refusal to produce the truth. It seems clear that small children act unself-consciously and unreflectively in the sense that they do not attach words to what they are doing, and depend for their ability to learn *how* to give such verbal accounts on linguistically more mature people *telling* them why they act as they do. After a time they begin to be able to tell *themselves* what others have told them, but not necessarily with any greater accuracy.

*Jeremy was a ten-year-old in the care of the Local Authority. He had spent the first two hours of one particular morning barricaded in his room, systematically destroying every object in it, including the windows. Eventually he was extracted by the staff and subjected to a searching inquiry by three child care officers as to what was disturbing him. Anxiously concerned, gently and without any threat, they asked him in every way they knew how why he had done it, what was worrying him. They racked their brains to present him with possible alternative explanations, but always with a request for his affirmation or denial. In other words, they were absolutely convinced that he knew the explanation for his conduct, and that he could in principle put that knowledge into words. However, it seemed clear from his expression of pain, confusion and bewilderment that Jeremy had not the slightest idea why he had acted as he had. What he desperately needed (and did not get) was someone to* tell *him why, so that he himself could acquire a verbal purchase on his anguish. (*Telling *someone the reasons for his or her actions, or the nature of his or her feelings, is one of the most difficult and easily abused responsibilities of loving.)*

Honest reflection on one's experience would, I should have thought, strongly suggest that the situation with adults is little different from that with children. The explanations we offer for our actions are no more than accounts which may or may not be accurate, but which have no special claim to truth simply because they are given by the person whose conduct is in question. This becomes most clear in those situations where our professed intentions are at odds with our fundamental desires. The man who has promised himself and others to give up smoking might, at the end of a desperate day without cigarettes, tell himself that he is going to take the dog for a walk. As it happens, he walks the dog past an off-licence where he 'decides' to buy a can of beer for himself and a bar of chocolate for his children. As he makes these purchases, he impulsively buys a packet of cigarettes, telling himself that if he has a packet in the house it will calm his agitation even though he will leave them untouched. Half an hour after arriving back home he 'decides' that just one cigarette will relieve the withdrawal symptoms sufficiently to enable him to get through the following day without smoking. His massive dishonesty would of course be apparent to anybody who watched him, and quite possibly his wife knew from his first expression of altruistic interest in the dog what his true intention was.

Most of the time, perhaps, our conduct is sufficiently free of conflict for us to be able to provide a relatively accurate commentary upon it, and this can easily lend plausibility to the belief that the commentary (which is likely to be replete with terms such as 'decision', 'intention', etc.) somehow precedes and even causes the conduct. It may only be at moments of despair, when conflict has driven us into a position which we had sworn to ourselves never to occupy, that we catch a glimpse of the disjunction between actions and words. In fact, I think, we are in no better position than anyone else to say why we do what we do. We, as they, must 'read off' the reasons for our actions, the intentions saturating our conduct, from the activity itself, and since we may often have a greater stake than they in the valuation placed upon our conduct, our interpretation of it may have a much weaker claim to truth than theirs.

That people's own accounts of their actions have any particularly privileged claim to accuracy has long been rejected by most psychologists, and it is now quite well established through carefully conducted experiments that people can perform complex intellectual tasks, or skilfully execute highly sophisticated intentional activity, without having any conscious awareness of how they do it (i.e., without being able to put it into words), although they might be quite ready to give more or less plausible accounts which they themselves feel convinced are true.* It is also, of course, one of Freud's greatest claims to fame that he showed how people could be utterly unaware of the determinants of their actions, and he argued quite explicitly that the motives which lurk in our 'unconscious minds' lurk there not least because we manage not to attach to them words which accurately describe them.

However, in our everyday dealings with each other we tend to have an unquestioning faith that, unless people choose to lie, the verbal explanations they give of their actions and motives are the most reliable indications we have of what they actually are up to. Even our most revered institutions, as, for example, the legal system, depend often on this assumption – although witnesses may be called to cast doubt on defendants' veracity, it is frequently assumed that the latter could give a true explanation of their actions if they chose to, unless, perhaps, they were 'suffering from' 'insanity'. It is thus a widespread assumption throughout our culture that a person's activity is the result of a process of deliberation in which, before embarking upon any particular course, he or she draws upon a kind of cerebral commentary in order to 'decide' what to do. No doubt we are

---

* A particularly interesting, though technical, account of much of this experimental work is given in R. E. Nisbett and T. D. Wilson, Telling more than we can know: verbal reports on mental processes, *Psychological Review*, 1977, vol. 84, pp. 231–59.

misled in this by virtue of the fact that the only way we have of communicating in any kind of analytic detail about our conduct is through words – even sports coaches or teachers of music are forced to rely heavily on words in order to make available to reflection the utterly inarticulate performances of their pupils. It is thus easily, if naively, concluded that, say, an accomplished batsman is guiding his actions with a similar, though internal, kind of commentary, when in fact, of course, everything happens far too quickly to allow of any such possibility; he can only criticize his performance verbally *after* the event.

As a general rule, then, we assume that if a person gives us an account of his actions which he sincerely believes to be the case (i.e., he is not lying) this is the best guide we have as to the true state of affairs. It is the prevalence of this myth which makes possible the phenomenon of self-deception. That people are capable of 'kidding themselves' is of course something widely acknowledged in our culture, though I suspect that this possibility is considered only in relatively rare and fairly superficial cases; what we do not recognize, I think, is that self-deception is the characteristic mode of existence in this society, nor that it is the combination of self-deception and our excessive over-valuation of words which maintain the objectifying structures of our culture.

To say that people deceive themselves is not to question the sincerity of their utterances – the element of dishonesty in self-deception exists more at the level of experience than at that of words. Indeed, dishonesty may not itself be the best concept to invoke in this context: on the whole, people deceive themselves through lack of courage rather than lack of honesty, or even simply through lack of clarity about the predicament in which they find themselves – one may deceive oneself because one lacks the courage to face the implications of one's experience, or simply because that experience is so confused and puzzling that one opts for a relatively non-threatening interpretation of it. But in either case there is no doubt that people believe the stories they tell themselves.

*Janet had become an increasingly frequent visitor to her general practitioner over the course of two years or so. She complained of violent headaches, dizzy spells and bouts of vomiting. She had been examined by several specialists and tried on a wide variety of medicines, but all to no avail. The doctor's suspicion that her complaints were 'neurotic in origin' increased in proportion to the imperviousness of her symptoms to the usual treatments, and he therefore inquired after her psychological well-being — whether anything might be worrying her at home, etc. Janet immediately perceived what was in his mind, and angrily repudiated any suggestion that her symptoms were 'psychological' or 'imaginary'. The situation deteriorated when a friend of Janet's mother-in-law died suddenly of a brain tumour, some of the symptoms of which had been dizziness and vomiting — Janet became convinced that she had a tumour herself, and insisted on seeing a neurologist. Like the other specialists she had consulted, he also found no physical abnormality, and suggested to her general practitioner that Janet's symptoms were indeed 'neurotic'. Once again, the doctor's — this time slightly more insistent — inquiries into her psychological circumstances revealed nothing of significance.*

*Janet, as he knew, had been married for five years, and had two little boys, one four and the other two years old, of whom she was very fond (the doctor knew she looked after them well, bringing them to the surgery when they needed medical attention, etc., and he also knew that her home was well kept and carefully looked after). Her husband was a self-employed joiner, and worked very hard, and successfully, to provide for his family — he was in the process of building up his business, had recently taken on two workers, and in fact was making quite a lot of money. Janet was always smartly dressed, and had a new car of her own. Neither she nor her doctor could find anything in these circumstances to suggest that her symptoms were 'psychological', but he nevertheless persuaded her, considerably against her will, to see a clinical psychologist.*

*Interviews with the psychologist – about an hour every fortnight – extended over a period of eighteen months. At first Janet talked most about her symptoms, and there was no doubting her fear that she might have a brain tumour, nor that she viewed the hypothesis that the symptoms were 'psychological' with hostile scepticism. The picture she had given her general practitioner of a happy domestic life was also at first that which she painted for the psychologist. However, it emerged over the weeks that a rather different view could be taken.*

*Her own family background had not, it transpired, been a happy one (though Janet's initial statement had been that 'you couldn't have a better Mum and Dad'). She had felt dominated by what she saw as a more successful sister who was the apple of, in particular, her father's eye. Her mother was a worrying, uncertain person, cowed by her husband, who himself drank heavily and had been periodically violent towards both Janet and her mother, though never her sister. It took Janet some weeks to acknowledge that she had been miserably unhappy in this household, and that the feelings she bore both her father and her sister bordered on hatred. She still felt close to her mother, and visited her often during the daytime, when her father was at work. It was evident to the psychologist that Janet felt extremely guilty at voicing (putting into words) the feelings she had so long avoided confronting.*

*She had married at the age of eighteen, largely, as she now saw it, to escape from home, but also because she was moved by her husband's affection for her, scarcely able to believe that anyone could prefer her to her sister. It took several months before the psychologist could gain a clear view of her marital situation: at first she represented it to him as almost ideal. After an initially happy time, her husband became increasingly preoccupied with his work, and she only saw him briefly late in the evening or on Sundays. Her two small children she found extremely demanding, and sole responsibility for their welfare made her anxious; she worried about shouting at them too often. She spent as much time as she could with her mother, who seemed by now to be her only source of support. As Janet grew to trust the psychologist, and indeed to allow herself to review her own experience, she revealed further details of her life – for example, that on two or three occasions, when feeling at her loneliest and most despairing, she had been to bed with her husband's best friend when he had called round during the day. This seemed to have done little for her other than make her feel guilty. Very soon after she had begun to confront her painful experience, Janet's concern about her symptoms began to diminish, though from time to time there would be a resurgence of anxiety about them, often, it seemed to the psychologist, when she was about to come face-to-face with further unpalatable truths.*

Now it could not plausibly be maintained that, at the time she consulted her general practitioner, Janet did not in *some* sense 'know' about her unhappy family background, her loneliness in her marriage, her affair with her husband's friend, and so on. What was also clear, however, was that she *genuinely believed* that her physical sensations (of anxiety) were in fact symptoms of an illness, which her mother-in-law's friend's death eventually persuaded her to be a brain tumour. In fact, Janet restricted her knowledge of her predicament to what she *told herself* about it. She was not, so to speak, critical of her experience. After all, her mother and father and sister were features of an *unquestionable* experience which constituted her reality – they were her family, and one is supposed to love and honour one's family. She had no first-hand knowledge of what else a family could be. Similarly, her husband was doing only what husbands are supposed to do, and for her to take seriously her unhappiness would have been to raise questions which could not be raised without the most threatening and painful implications, and though her brief affair constituted an attempt to assuage her loneliness, it formed a part of her conduct which, again, did not have to be reflected upon with words. She could preserve her normality, her existence within the world in which everyone is expected to live, simply by not attending reflectively to her actual experience of it. She was married to a man who was by all standards doing his best for her and their children; there was no other life obviously available to her, no situation she could envisage which offered greater happiness without causing enormous distress to others and herself. Her pain and confusion thus demanded an explanation which, though apparently not to be found in the natural, immediate usualness of her day-to-day existence, was from her point of view afforded much more adequately by the hypothesis that she had a brain tumour.

As long as we restrict what we 'know' to what we are pre-pared to tell ourselves, we can (at the cost, of course, of some considerable discomfort) preserve the myths by which we wish to live. Our culture almost invites us to take a stance of bad faith towards our experience, since it provides us with a com-mon verbal currency which is designed to protect us from the dangers and risks of subjectivity. In Janet's case, for example, there was no particular community for her to turn to which could provide for her a context in which to examine critically her experience. There was nothing so outlandish about her background or her marriage or her situation as mother (indeed, I have deliberately described a 'case' which typifies the exist-ence of countless women) which seemed to justify pain on the scale she felt it. Our 'objective' standards would indicate, in fact, that she was particularly advantaged in relation to the majority of her social peers – she had a 'decent' upbringing and a 'good', hard-working husband and 'two lovely children', and she was financially well off. Having, as it were, put obstacles in the way of her analysing her situation according to her actual experience of it, however, the objectifying culture does provide alternative concepts by which it may be 'understood', e.g., through the concept of 'illness'. It takes particular courage and tenacity in these circumstances to reject the ready-made, objective framework in which one may conceptualize one's difficulties, and to advance instead an analysis based upon one's own subjective position.

To take a stance of good faith towards one's experience, to take heed of one's intuitive sensitivity, is to assert the values of subjectivity and to challenge the thick, heavy, objectifying verbal concepts which monopolize our reality. The emperor's mythical clothes are woven with words, and their close, heavy texture can be unpicked only through a courageous, isolating and often painful attempt to make articulate what one senses to be the case without becoming enmeshed in concepts already in the service of myth. Perhaps this is why those philosophers and others who have written in support of the subjective are so difficult – for the Anglo-Saxon mind, at least – to grasp: it is as if they need to dodge and duck their way between the ponderous, pinning-down objectifications of our common conceptual language in order to provide subtlety and space for the development of subjective insights. But this is not the concern only of philosophers: as I shall argue in the next chapter, our very anxiety is at least in part an insistence that our experience be taken seriously, a symbolic expression of the fact that our everyday language is not capable of taking true account of our pain.

There is no way of saying much of what we sense and feel, and it is probably our culture as much as ourselves which determines what *can* be said (in this respect Freud was perhaps unfair in emphasizing so strongly the role of the *individual* in repression – i.e. in detaching words from actions – and suggesting that this is largely a pathological process). In fact, though we live, deceptively and self-deceptively, in a construction of reality depending heavily on our conscious, verbal accounts of it, our conduct towards one another, indeed our transactions with the world as a whole, take place very largely without the use of words. In this respect we are not so different from other animals as we think. A number of concepts which are built into our everyday language make it very difficult for us to appreciate the significance of this state of affairs – most of us see language as simply describing things, and fail to notice that it may embody an entire philosophy which is utterly misleading. Again, it may only be at moments of particular conflict or distress that one becomes aware that ordinary language does not do justice to experience.

For example, one particularly important area in which our everyday concepts fail us – and one which it is essential to clarify if we are to achieve any understanding of psychological distress – is that surrounding the idea of responsibility.

The attraction of self-deception is so great not least because the main alternative to seeing our distress as somehow inflicted upon us – as, for example, 'illness' – is to see it as being our 'fault'. Our language certainly affords us the possibility of being objective bodies open to attack by malign organisms or prone to mechanical defect, and on the whole illness carries no imputation of blame. Over the last hundred and fifty years or so, more and more 'behaviour' which was once seen as the individual's personal responsibility has been redefined as the effect of illness – for example (quite apart from actions definable as arising out of 'insanity'), alcoholism, some kinds of sexual aberration, and even some forms of criminality. Naughty children may now be seen as 'suffering from' 'behaviour disorders'. In part one can see the value of this kind of view – it is more humane than the otherwise punitive attitude which may be taken towards deviant conduct, and maybe, even, it contains a tacit acknowledgment of the fact that people are frequently at a loss to account for their own actions. But it is precisely this assumption – that if 'behaviour' is not 'caused' by, for example, illness, then the person must be able to account for it – which leads us into difficulty. As long as we believe that people's ordinary activity is carried out in response to a kind of internal monologue in which decisions are taken, intentions settled upon and consequences calculated, we are likely to conclude that when their conduct takes an undesirable course it has done so because of their deliberate perversity. If, in these circumstances, they insist on withholding from us an account of or an acknowledgment of their wrong-doing, we are likely to assume that they are compounding their guilt by lying or malingering.

Thus the patient who consults her doctor about acutely distressing symptoms of physical dis-ease, when told that these have 'no organic cause', is forced to consider the imputation inherent in our conceptual system that she is 'imagining' them.

Many patients, having exhausted all the possibilities offered by physical medicine, say with a kind of hopeless despair, 'I know it must be me' or, 'I know it's my imagination', as if all they can reasonably expect (and, of course, they frequently get it from doctors of the 'old school') is a sharp reprimand or an exhortation to pull themselves together. But because they know that they cannot even tell *themselves* why they feel as they do, and because conceptually there seems no other possibility open to them, they continue secretly to believe that there *must* be some*thing* 'causing' their complaints.

If, however, the arguments put forward in this chapter can be accepted – i.e., that our conduct does *not* have to be within the reach of words – then a third possibility opens up: that we struggle to understand our actions in the same way that we struggle to understand anybody else's; we try to see what reasons we might have for acting the way we do, 'read off' our intentions from our activity without assuming that we must know in advance what they are. This, certainly, implies an acknowledgment that our conduct is indeed our own, and nobody else's, and that the reasons for it are our reasons, and hence that we are responsible for what we do. But the concepts of 'fault' and 'blame', I think, legitimately apply only in situations where we do indeed know what we are doing, and *that* what we are doing is socially disapproved of. It is of course much easier to be aware *that* we are doing something than to be aware of *why* we are doing it. Thus in these situations, and in *some* respects, we can give an accurate commentary on our conduct. In most cases at least, when I park on the yellow lines I could give a clear account of what I'm doing, and how, though I know the significance of yellow lines, I calculate that in the ten minutes I intend to stay parked there no traffic warden or policeman is likely to pass by – if one does, I can scarcely claim diminished responsibility or maintain that I am not to blame. In this way, the law defines for us those situations in which we must take care to spell out *some* of the (social) rules applicable to our actions, and, indeed, limits itself by and large to those situations in which we can. In contrast, when driven by inarticulate terror to run screaming from an enormous bloated spider advancing across the carpet, I have no such coherent account to give of my actions (nor is there any *social* necessity for one), though I am still responsible for running and screaming, for these are nobody's actions but my own. Thus fault and blame are concepts relevant to situations in which we know *that* we are breaking rules in a *social* context.

To extend these concepts into the psychological sphere, by, for example, implicating them in a demand that we know *why* we are doing something, is neither useful nor legitimate.

The attitude which it is reasonable to adopt to the kind of responsibility I am trying to elucidate here is not one of blame, but rather one of interest, tolerance and concern. I presumably have my reasons for being afraid of spiders, and they may well be understandable; I am certainly not wilfully withholding them either from myself or anyone else, and I should actually quite like to know what they are.

Of course, 'spider phobia' is a fairly common phenomenon, and although one may feel rather silly about it from time to time, it is unlikely to make one feel a social outcast. Many people who find themselves tortured by either more severe or less familiar forms of anxiety, however, feel that, unless a suitably exonerating 'illness' explanation can be found, their apparently irrational fears – quite apart from being open to construction as their own 'fault' – render them absurd. This may again be put down to the myth that others are 'normal' and act always according to a coherent (verbalizable) analysis of their situation. Perhaps the anxious person's shame at his or her supposed 'difference' from others would be lessened by the realization that all of us, most of the time, do not know why we are doing what we are doing.

The fact that any kind of answer is difficult to give does not mean that it is idle to inquire into why we do what we do, for in making such an inquiry we may begin to grasp the importance of our subjective stance in the world. Accepting responsibility for our conduct merely means that we acknowledge that we have reasons for it, and that those reasons are ours. This at least has the merit of ruling out the possibility that they are anybody else's reasons, or that, as passive objects, we are caused to do what we do by external forces. We thus remove one of the prevailing myths of an objectifying culture – i.e., that our conduct is *determined* by causes outside ourselves which can be revealed only through scientific analysis by appropriately qualified experts. Even our most incomprehensible actions, it may turn out, are the result neither of our badness nor madness (nor even helplessness) but rather arise from a perfectly reasonable and understandable construction (our construction) of our experience, even though that construction is lived out in our activity rather than transmitted through the medium of words.

In seeing how this can be the case, however, our language is once again sadly inadequate to the task. Most of the difficulty seems to stem from our deeply ingrained habit of thinking of mind and body as two qualitatively different kinds of thing, in which the latter depends for its proper functioning on the instructions of the former. Before, that is, the body can actually be got physically into motion, it is felt that something must be wished, or wanted, or decided by the mind, and, as I have already suggested, it is further often felt that the wishing and wanting and deciding which take place do so in some kind of verbal manner, or at least in a manner which can potentially be put into words. In this way we are led to suppose that we are in control of our bodies as a crane driver is in control of his crane, and that if we want to know the significance of our conduct, all we have to do is consult ourselves. Hence the puzzlement of people who 'find themselves' doing unaccountable things, or unable to do 'obviously' desirable things. It is, for example, characteristic of people gripped by anxiety that they may feel compelled to do things which they don't 'want' to do, or incapable of 'deciding' to do things which would appear clearly to benefit them. The severely 'phobic' housewife cannot, surely, *want* to live the life of a recluse, but though she sees the advantages of leaving the house to do essential shopping, she cannot 'decide' to open the front door, although that is what she 'wants' to do. If the crane appears to behave irrationally, it makes sense to inquire into the reasons from the driver, for here person and machine (mind and body) are indeed two separate entities, the one controlling the other. But one may harangue an anxiously conflicted individual endlessly without becoming any the wiser as to the reasons for his or her conduct. Nor is it that such people are exceptional by virtue of their predicament: in fact, they provide particularly clear examples of what is the case with all of us, and demonstrate the futility of our adopting an inquisitorial attitude to ourselves in seeking the explanation of our conduct. The language of 'explanation', in which the individual inquires into his or her own wants, wishes, intentions, decisions, etc., is a maze of hopeless confusion.

A person's desires, wants, decisions, etc., cannot be separated from their *bodily* enactment. We can only talk as we do about such concepts by abstracting them from the physical structures of which they are a part, and falsely turning them into non-physical objects. This is a point well recognized by psychologists, particularly those of the 'behavioural' school; their mistake, however, was to conclude that because, say, 'purposes' could not be seen as non-physical *things* there could be no meaning to the term 'purpose' which was not reducible to something much more 'scientific' like 'behaviour', which could itself be seen simply as the 'response' to 'stimuli'. However, it is not the case that 'behaviour', or as I prefer to call it, conduct, cannot be seen as purposive, but merely that purpose cannot be abstracted from what people *do*. The woman who claims that she really *wants* to go out shopping when actually she always stays indoors is not taking full enough account of her conduct. The only way one can really be clear about what one wants is to look at what one does. Presumably she claims to 'want' to go out since that would accord best with what she thinks she *ought* to be doing, but in making the claim she fails to recognize that in fact being terrified is a very good reason for *not* wanting to go out, even though not going out has clear disadvantages of its own. While going out would solve some problems (and is therefore to that extent desirable) it would create considerably worse ones, not least of which would be the person's becoming inundated with fear. There is therefore nothing either shameful or puzzling in concluding that the fact that she stays in suggests that the 'phobic' person does *not* want to go out. Once this is agreed, she can perhaps begin to see that her conduct is not simply crazy or wilfully bad, but actually forms part of a stance she is taking for reasons which are perfectly understandable. We must read off the nature of our desires and purposes from the conduct in which we find ourselves engaged. To do this we need, as suggested before, an attitude towards ourselves of interest, tolerance and concern, in which it is far more fruitful, and indeed accurate, to assume the fundamental rationality of our conduct than it is to anticipate its moral reprehensibility. There is no shame attached to not knowing why one does what one does, and indeed no special credit to be accorded the person who can give an instant explanation.

As with 'wanting', so with 'deciding'. Many people feel alarmed at the idea that their activity is anything other than the outcome of a carefully monitored series of decisions, and their alarm can reach panic proportions if they find, as they are likely to, that at times of stress the control which normally they seem to have over what they do suddenly evaporates. But here again it is the 'abnormal' experience which points to the true state of affairs. I do not feel that there is any convincing case to be made for our activity's being the result of decisions which we settle upon from time to time as we conduct our internal deliberations. Our activity is or is not itself decisive, and our decisions are made in and through our conduct. The anxious woman who hovers inside her front door waiting for a 'decision' to go out is in fact *acting* indecisively, and the 'decision' to go out is only made as the activity itself is carried out. We can indeed abstract decisions from our embodied activity in order to talk about them, but we cannot *make* them in this way – no amount of talking to oneself can constitute a decision. Decisions come into being with their bodily enactment. Again, because we do not first 'make' decisions somewhere inside our heads before we actually act 'upon' them, this does not mean that our conduct must be somehow impulsive and unpredictable (which is a fear difficult to shake off if one is wedded to the 'internal commentary' theory), for it is not only language which is ordered and rational. The pianist's activity is no less controlled, purposive or decisive for being unattached to words. Here again we are easily misled by the 'crane driver' model of behaviour: if the crane were suddenly to start doing things *not* instructed by its driver, one could of course reasonably view its movements as in a sense dangerously irrational. But to account for our own conduct we neither need nor have 'drivers' sitting inside our heads telling us what to do; and, as many others have pointed out, even if we had it would solve no problems, for then we should have to account for how our 'decision maker' makes its decisions (presumably by having another 'decision maker' sitting inside *its* head), and so on and on.

Appraising, wanting, intending and deciding are all accomplished through our total embodied activity, in which verbal reflection plays a relatively insignificant part. If we want to achieve a verbal understanding of our conduct we must observe very attentively what we do. And if our available vocabulary is found inadequate to the task, or fails to do justice to what we see, or imposes upon us conceptual structures which distort our experience, we shall simply have to struggle to refine it.

I am convinced that these are no mere abstract or empty philosophical issues. Our inarticulate subjectivity is at work constructing our lives and our world at every level of social organization, while our objectifying linguistic culture is busy articulating an almost entirely mythical version of what we are about. Language here becomes the tool of bad faith, its central function to deceive. At least in part the explanation for this is to

be found in the defensive function of objectivity – its myths
protect us from the threat, the pain, and the sheer hard work of
getting to grips with what we actually do to and with each
other. It is easy often for the psychotherapist to see this process
at work in individuals, and to some extent, perhaps, to correct
it. For example, the man who claims that all he wants to do to
achieve lasting happiness is gain promotion at work, when in
fact his every action sabotages that possibility, may be made
aware that he has a deeper project of failure which is in fact
much more important to him than is his avowed aim. At more
complex levels of social organization the same processes may be
seen at work, though here it is less easy, but (desperately)
more important, to become aware of them: governments, for
example, assure their national populations, as well as each
other, of their peaceful intentions, while at the same time
moving towards the most aggressive and destructive (and self-
destructive) confrontation imaginable. The child who knows
that the emperor is naked also knows that the man of peace
does not build an arsenal. If the analysis in this chapter is
correct, the most terrifying possibility is opened up: it is not
simply that governments are lying, or bluffing (or, indeed,
deterring), or can be trusted to be in some kind of skilled control
over their projects, but that they may be *deceived* about the
aims of what *they themselves* are doing. Again, just as the
individual can disclaim responsibility for acting upon the
*reasons* for his or her conduct and can change them, through
the obliging offices of objectifying language, into 'causes' which
he or she 'cannot help', so societies can blind themselves to the
institutions and interests ('pressure groups', etc.) which, *out of
their awareness*, shape their policies. As the individual needs to
wake up to his or her intentions by reading them off from his or
her conduct, so collectively we need to see that our activities
may betoken something quite other than what we *sincerely*
avow, and that unknown to ourselves we might have the most
appalling aims. The only way we can criticize or communicate
about what we are, as subjects, making of ourselves and our
world is to establish between our language and our experience
a relation of good faith.

The conceptual vocabulary of objectivity, as has been
observed by several critics of contemporary society,* pushes us

---

* See for example E. Fromm, *To Have or to Be*, Jonathan Cape, 1978. Also,
I. Illich, *Tools for Conviviality*, Calder and Boyars, 1973.

more and more in the direction of seeing ourselves as containers or owners of objectified forces which, so to speak, pursue their own existence within us (rather as one might envisage the crane-driving decision maker doing). Partly this has come about through the gradual conversion of verbs – i.e. words to do with activity – into nouns. Thus, being unable to do something becomes 'having a problem', wanting something becomes 'having a need', making love becomes 'having sex', and being good at something becomes 'having a skill'. The human being thus becomes a kind of box of tricks (some good, some bad), a programmable automaton in which the needs, problems, skills, etc., can be slotted in or out like floppy discs in a computer.

The project to mechanize people (to which I shall give more detailed attention in a later chapter) represents the ultimate in objectification, and certainly, if successful, would absolve us from the demands of responsibility and the terrors of subjectivity. But we can assent to it, and to its manifestation in the use of language, only by standing to our experience in a relation of bad faith. Paradoxically perhaps, it is particularly in those situations where we are said to have 'broken down' that the inadequacies of our objectifying concepts are most apparent, and where the inescapability of our subjectivity is revealed. At these times, if we are honest, we may be able to see and accept that our conduct is constituted by our own assessment of and responsible reaction to our situation in the world, however painful that situation is, and however wordless our reaction to it. This is obviously not to suggest that we deserve what we get or that the individual is responsible for the predicament which gives rise to his or her fear and pain. The evils of the world are absolutely real, and not to be wished away as the maladjustment of individual people. How we deal with them, however, is up to us, personally and collectively. There is no 'them' to whom the job can safely be left.

# 5   The Language of Anxiety

In using our everyday language and the concepts embedded in it, we tell each other and ourselves more or less what we want to hear. The comfortably familiar, objective and objectifying verbal structures with which we surround ourselves are designed to reinforce the myths by which we live and reassure us that the boat in which we all find ourselves, even if it rocks a bit at times, is fundamentally under firm (objective) guidance and control. If, occasionally, we find ourselves feeling more than usually queasy, this is likely to be regarded as the result of a malfunction somewhere in the system (most probably in the individual's 'adjustment' to the world) which, given the requisite expert attention, can quite likely be put right fairly painlessly.

The two chapters following this one will deal in greater detail with the ways in which our society meets the threat of psychological distress – and in particular anxiety – but here I want to consider first the possibility that the kind of 'symptoms' of which people complain are not merely indications of something's having gone wrong which can be put right, but rather are forms arising out of people's *experience* of the world, and constitute almost a language on their own, though a subjective rather than an objective one. Acute distress and anxiety are such ubiquitous and pervasive phenomena in these times that they can scarcely be dismissed as in some sense unnatural, unfortunate hiccups in the smooth running of our everyday lives, and I believe they are to be taken seriously, not by our trying to eliminate them as mechanical defects in an otherwise satisfactory system, but rather by attending closely to their *significance*.

It strikes me as a surprising fact that, although they have identified some of the most important features of 'symptoms' of distress, psychologists and others have failed to recognize the implications of their own observations. For example, 'neurotic symptoms' have (unlike symptoms of physical illness) been characterized as *learned* phenomena by a wide range of psychological writers, and as *symbolic* phenomena by, in particular, psychoanalytic thinkers. However, though, as I shall argue shortly, I think both these characteristics *are* typical of the phenomena in question, the latter have continued to be treated by almost all concerned *as if* they were curable symptoms. In other words, though many people have seen clearly that these 'symptoms' have features which make them quite unlike the kinds of symptoms of illness with which we are more familiar (like, for example, the symptoms of a common cold), they have nevertheless been so caught up in the 'symptom' analogy that they have continued to treat them as if the very features they have remarked upon do not exist. It seems to have escaped the notice of nearly all psychologists and psychiatrists that, for example, 'treatment' is not an appropriate procedure to apply either to symbolic or to learned phenomena, even when they have acknowledged that such is the nature of 'symptoms'. So great is the power of our myths that even when their falsity is laid bare we continue to be ruled by them. In this case, it seems, we simply cannot afford to give up the idea that anxiety is the remediable sign of mechanical breakdown, and so, in the manner typical of self-deception, we contrive not to pay attention to our own discoveries concerning its nature.

Far from being a mechanical fault, a 'symptom', a 'dysfunction' or an indication of 'maladjustment', the experience of anxiety constitutes an assertion of the real nature of our subjective engagement with the world. To fall prey to anxiety is, at least partially, to fall *out* of self-deception, since the phenomenon of anxiety is an insistence that the subject's experience be taken seriously, that the person's *actual* predicament cannot and will not be ignored.

Were words really as powerful as we would like to make them, we could indeed manufacture an endless series of alternative worlds in which to live. Merely by inventing a new way of interpreting the world – verbally remodelling it, so to speak – we could magic away any painful circumstance in which we found ourselves (there are indeed forms of 'psychotherapy' which attempt to do precisely this, as we shall see in Chapter 7). Because different people have different perspectives on the world and describe it in different ways, and because the same person can also experience similar events in very different ways at different times, it is easy to be encouraged in thinking that there is no hard reality behind the seemingly infinite relativity of views which can be taken of it. But to suppose this would be as foolish as to suppose that, because we have free will, we could do *anything* we liked, and is to overlook the fact that, though we can describe an experience in very different ways and from many different perspectives, the experience has a reality of its own which cannot simply be talked away. The experience of anxiety indicates to us that there are features of our world which we can no longer afford to ignore. Nobody would suggest that the panic attendant upon your being charged by a bull in an open field would best be 'treated' by taking a tranquillizer, but rather that its prompting to you to take to your heels could usefully be heeded. Although anxiety has longer-lasting effects and less easily identifiable referents than does fear of charging bulls, its 'message' may not be all that dissimilar, and the threat to which it relates none the less real. Anxiety, I believe, tells us that the world is a place of real terrors which we ignore only at our greater peril. We mythify anxiety precisely because we do wish to ignore the terrors to which it points.

However clever we are at telling ourselves comforting stories, however sophisticated our ability to deceive ourselves, we actually *are* engaged *bodily* in a *real* world which cannot be wished (or talked) away. The evils of the world hurt us because they impinge upon our embodied existence, and they can be changed only through our embodied intervention in an actual world (not by 'thinking' of them in a different way, or by the 'treatment' of their effects on us through interference – either physical or mental – with the way we perceive them). Our involvement as subjects in an actual world affects us in ways we cannot escape, however unpalatable we might consider that involvement to be and however much we might wish it to be otherwise.

> *A married woman, referred because of her 'frigidity', confesses (or comes to see) after a time that she is not frigid at all, but is in love with someone other than her husband. 'But I don't want it to be like that,' she says, 'I don't want to have those feelings with Bill; I want to have them with my husband.'*

Our feelings, then, insist on recognition even though, in our accounts, we can dissemble endlessly. Although we can fake our experience through the way we describe it, and even if we can blind ourselves to its significance, we cannot fake the experience itself.

As suggested in the previous chapter, that we talk about things as being 'imaginary' or 'all in the mind', etc., is the unfortunate consequence of a misleading philosophical split between mind and body. This gives us the chance to see 'worries' as things which take place somewhere inside our heads, and thus as of little consequence, while actual bodily sensations are seen as mechanical events most properly the province of medicine. Thus worry becomes a phenomenon internal to the individual – perhaps 'imaginary' – and to be combated by, for example, positive thinking or pulling oneself together, while sensations of physical discomfort are to be dealt with by medication or surgery. In both cases it is quite easy to leave out of account the actual evils of the world which may well be – almost certainly are – playing a part; presumably these are to be coped with by those of us clear-sighted, level-headed and healthy enough to deal with them as 'problems'. To deal with anxiety as *either* mental (worry) *or* physical (illness) thus serves the myth that the evils of the world do not have the evil *effects* which in fact they do have (in giving rise, among other things, to the *meaningful* pain which is anxiety) and renders them as, *at worst*, practical 'problems' to be overcome in an otherwise well functioning system.

*Mrs Eliot has four children and an alcoholic husband who, though a pleasant and affectionate man when sober, can be verbally cruel and sexually brutal when drunk. They live in a small terraced council house on a 'problem' estate, and Mrs Eliot's neighbours are unremittingly noisy and aggressive. She has no close friends, and her relations with her own family are strained – her father used to beat her savagely, and her mother dealt with life by taking a submissive and thus rather ineffectual stance towards most difficulties; she is therefore little support to her daughter. Because of her childhood experience, Mrs Eliot's fundamental (inarticulate) view of herself is as worthless, and hence as extremely lucky to be taken notice of by anyone, however badly they might treat her. Two of Mrs Eliot's children are bed-wetters (though both she and her husband are clearly very fond of them, this is probably in part the consequence of the almost continuously high levels of tension in the household). Though he made good money when working, Mr Eliot has been unemployed for two years, and money is tight. Mrs Eliot works non-stop: shopping, cleaning, taking children to and from school, washing sheets, cooking for an endless succession of her husband's friends and relatives at all times of the day and night, managing the household budget as best she can, suffering the humiliation of those dependent upon the state for basic financial security. Occasionally she is overcome with 'symptoms' of anxiety (dizziness, headaches, breathing difficul-*

*ties, burning sensations, etc.) and, puzzled and frightened by what she takes to be signs of illness, she consults her general practitioner fairly frequently at these times. She was once diagnosed by a psychiatrist as an 'inadequate personality' and heavily tranquillized. Nobody, least of all herself, saw that, in view of the circumstances of her life and her living conditions, she was in fact coping with almost superhuman adequacy, and nobody made the connexion between what was happening to her and how she felt.*

Psychological distress and anxiety are of course bodily feelings – i.e., physical sensations *with a meaning*. They are neither imaginary ('in the mind') nor purely the result of mechanical breakdown, but expressive of a certain kind of embodied relation with the world. Sadness at the death of a loved person is not (yet!) considered a treatable illness, nor is the physical experience of ecstatic happiness (at, say, falling in love, or winning the pools) taken as an indication of madness. We are used in these circumstances to ascribing people's *feelings* to the particular form of their engagement with the world, but the demands of myth-preservation mean that we are quick to abandon the conferring of any such significance to the moods and feelings created by the intractable evils of our social organization. Somehow the Mrs Eliots are supposed to sort out their familial, marital, social, economic and housing (etc.) 'problems' without being seriously affected by them; if they are so affected, they are deemed to be 'inadequate' or 'ill'. Certainly, Mrs Eliot herself thought she ought to be able to cope, and *could not understand* why she felt so 'ill'.

All our feelings are *about* something, that is, are felt in relation to a real state of affairs or an actual experience. As the evening draws on, Mrs Eliot becomes increasingly tense waiting for her husband to return from the pub, because she can never be sure whether he will be sober, friendly and 'normal', slightly drunk and maddeningly, inappropriately (in view of her state of near exhaustion) jovial, or very drunk, shouting and wildly abusive. The tense anticipation with which she awaits his arrival is a *bodily* state – like everyone else, she experiences the world with her body, and, in view of her circumstances, there can be no mystery about the pain she experiences. Whatever the grounds on which one distinguishes signs and symptoms of illness from other kinds of distressed state, one cannot correctly advance the view that illnesses are so classifiable because of their physical characteristics – *all* ex-periences are physical, since it is with our bodies that we do the experiencing. It does of course seem to be possible that a person may become distressed solely because of *internal* mechanical (bodily) malfunctioning (as, for example – as far as one can tell – in the case of pre-senile dementia), but it is a grave mistake to suppose that *all* physical discomfort must originate in this kind of way. Human beings exist in a delicate and sensitive rela-tionship of mutual transaction with their surrounding world, which itself can only be experienced, or indeed altered, through bodily engagement with it. To 'medicalize' indications of pain and distress which arise *between* people and their world is, literally, to dislocate people from the context in which they live and to obscure from them the possibility of their acting *morally* on the world to improve it. The same mistake is made by choosing to locate the 'problem' in the way the person *sees* the world (i.e., in his or her own head). Thus, when distressed or anxious people say either, 'it must be illness because the pain is real' or, 'it must be my imagination because the doctor says I'm not ill', they are falling for one of our commoner myths – i.e., that psychological pain is not bodily pain.

There are other myths which help to make it possible for us to deceive ourselves about the nature of anxiety. One, already touched upon in Chapter 2 (p. 27) is what one might call 'the myth of spatio-temporal contiguity' – i.e., that one's sensations of anxiety must be immediately linked either in space or time to some kind of clearly definable stimulus. Thus it may be thought that you cannot possibly be afraid of something unless you know what that something is (that is, it is immediately present 'in your mind'), or at least unless that something is *there with* you at the time. Mrs Eliot, for example, might well say that she cannot understand why she should 'get these feelings' when she is sitting quietly in the empty house watching the tele-vision. To be overcome *then* with anxiety or feelings of distress, she might feel, must indicate that she is ill rather than anxious because 'there is nothing to be anxious about'. But, of course, Mrs Eliot's past and her future do not disappear simply because she is on the face of it able to have a moment's respite in the present. The pain of her parents' (at least perceived) rejection of her and, more importantly, the insecurity it generated, do not evaporate simply because she is in a different time and place, nor does the sickening dread occasioned by the near certainty of her husband's future drunken rage get blotted out (indeed, it is increased) by his temporary absence. These experiences and anticipations are part of the very structure of her body, and they do not go away just because she is 'not thinking' about them: that she does not rehearse her misery in words to herself does not mean that it ceases to be present in her embodied existence. Just as any chance event – a sight or sound, for instance – can remind one of a current, or even past preoccupation, so a word, a gesture (even something on the television!) can bring one face to face with the *state* of dread in which one lives.

There are schools of psychotherapy which attempt to use a variant of the 'spatio-temporal contiguity' myth to avoid the inconveniences caused by the fact that we are subjective beings engaged in a *moral* relation with our world. What we should do, these 'humanistic' psychotherapists suggest, is learn to live in 'the now', 'fully and richly experiencing' the world immediately present to us, shaking off our morbid preoccupation with the past and our gloomy anticipation of a future which might never happen. But this lotus-eating philosophy again takes us out of relation to our world just as surely as the 'medicalizing' approach, and at least implicitly denies our moral concern, since the latter simply could not exist without an acute sense of past and future. For instance, the moral subject recognizes that if a painful past is not automatically to be reduplicated in the future, some *person* will have to intervene. (It is interesting to reflect in this context that some parents insist on their children suffering the same privations that they did while others are determined to use their experience to shape a less painful world for their children. I would speculate that the former are among those who place their faith in the objective correctness of our institutions, while the latter accept the importance of their subjective role.) This kind of 'humanistic' therapy thus advocates, albeit unwittingly, a kind of solipsistic self-indulgence which makes the individual an end in him or herself, and the future of the world an irrelevance.

There are other questions raised by Mrs Eliot's predicament to which we need to pay attention – for example, why does she, particularly in view of the fact that in terms of capacity for hard work and practical ability she is by no means incapable, put up with her lot with such apparent docility? The 'experts' will quite likely point to her lack of 'social skills' and 'assertiveness' and may suggest 'programmes' of 'training' to make good the 'deficits'. But here again, I think, we find ourselves in the world of myth, dealing this time with a version of the myth of 'cure'.

Those who advocate the overcoming of 'problems' through appropriate courses of 'training' would probably reject the idea that they are in fact caught up in the myth of cure, and would want to point out that theirs, far from being a medical approach, is one based on psychological ideas concerning the nature of learning (Chapter 7 will deal with some of these issues in greater detail). However, 'official' psychological ideas about learning are on the whole far from enlightening, and have paid almost no attention to features of learning which are starkly obvious to the most casual reflection. Because psychological views of learning as applied in the field of 'mental health' rest largely on the theory that people learn through a process of 'conditioning' (i.e., the automatic establishment of habitual connexions between 'stimuli' and 'responses') it seems to follow that people can be 'deconditioned' and 'reconditioned' if the original 'conditioned responses' turn out to have unfortunate or unwanted consequences. It thus becomes possible to think that Mrs Eliot could be put through a course of training which would replace her old faulty and inadequate ways of coping with her 'problems' with new and more effective habits. This, I think, is as an approach scarcely distinguishable from more overtly mechanistic notions of cure or repair, in which the person is seen basically as a machine which can be adjusted to optimal functioning through the requisite expert tinkering.

Mrs Eliot does indeed live her life the way she does because of what she has learned. But what she has learned she has learned as a living, embodied subject in a difficult and often cruel world, and the significance of her experience is unlikely to be erased or eroded through intervention based on the inane theories and practices of those indoctrinated by a half-baked and myth-infused 'official' psychology.

Some of the earliest lessons which Mrs Eliot learned were those which taught her insecurity. For reasons already explored in earlier chapters, she cannot rehearse those lessons in words, but her body knows the feeling of living under the Other's cold and rejecting eye. She does not complain about her lot because she sees no reason to: the worthless have no right to complain, and it is easy to see (though, of course, she could not say it) that Mrs Eliot counts herself lucky that *any* man should take an interest in her, and that her children do not openly revile her for the useless reject she knows herself to be. It will take more than a course in 'assertiveness training' from some brightly confident, earnest young psychologist to convince Mrs Eliot that the world is not a place which can easily do without her, and that the best thing she can do is stay inconspicuous and get what appreciation she can through service to others.

In talking about learning, psychologists have failed to take note of learning's nature. One learns insecurity in the same way that one learns to swim or to speak English. Even though one's ability may get a little rusty with time, one does not forget how to do the breast-stroke, nor can one be 'deconditioned' from knowing English or, for example, 'cured' of riding bicycles. One learns through committing oneself bodily to an engagement with the world, and the very structures of one's body are changed thereby. Though you might live abroad all your life and never meet a fellow countryman, it is likely to be your mother tongue which comes to your aid at times of pain or stress, or forms the words you whisper on your deathbed. Similarly, the person who knows the annihilating blows which the Other can deal is likely to be thrown into an all too familiar state of dread whenever life ceases to run more or less smoothly.

The myth that we can with ease free ourselves of the lessons of the past is constantly reiterated and reinforced by our official institutions as well as by the organs of popular entertainment. How many film or television villains, for example, are talked out of their black past and evil ways in a five-minute chat with a wise priest, a well-meaning policeman or a worldly-wise, tough-but-loving *pater familias*? Even though they must know better, haunting the back of many psychotherapists' minds, I bet, is the seductively magical idea that wise, or clever, or technically brilliant words will change patients' lives. This myth lurks behind the search for, and offer of, a thousand kinds of cure, from those of the conventional doctor to the faith healer, the brain surgeon to the spiritual guru. Behaviour therapists, hypnotists, counsellors of every kind and description, psychiatrists and psychologists, teachers, advisers, dieticians, experts in meditation and relaxation, all make the same implicit offer – to rid you of your experience of a painful world. If I am right when I suggest that we can no more be cured of insecurity than we can of knowing English, then it seems clear that that offer is bogus.

The anxious or insecure person has good reasons for feeling that way: reasons which spring from his or her bodily engagement in a real world and which will not for long remain obscured, however thick the blanket of myth which covers them. This is not to say that one can do nothing about the reasons for one's dread, only that the solution to the 'problems' they pose is not to be found in somehow juggling the individual's interpretation or perception of his or her experience. Though such juggling may usefully and validly form *part* of a process in which people begin to gain a subjective purchase on their predicament, it is, in the end, their actual embodied relation with their circumstances which counts. And, even then, new experience does not obliterate old. If a naturally acquired knowledge of English ceases to serve your needs, or if the crawl becomes more essential to your purposes than the breast-stroke, you may commit yourself to a relatively difficult and effortful process of learning a more appropriate language, or the new stroke, but in doing so you will not lose your former abilities. Our bodies do not acquire experience as does magnetic tape, but rather than being erased our earlier and more fundamental experiences provide the foundations on which (and the framework in which) later experience is built. Thus people whose insecurity is fundamental to their experience will, except perhaps in only the most unusual of circumstances, almost certainly *never* become fundamentally secure, though they may come to be able to acknowledge their insecurity in ways which mitigate its intensity and minimize the effects it has on the actual conduct of their lives.

The view that insecurity, and the anxiety it gives rise to, are acquired states of being rather than curable 'symptoms', and are as indelible as other learned acquisitions such as language or physical accomplishments like swimming or riding bicycles, has not occurred to me solely as the result of any kind of theoretical reflection, but has been imposed upon me as the result of my experience, particularly, but not by any means only, with patients. As part of a bureaucratic system of hospital treatment (which was for many years my role) it was easy to persuade oneself that patients who came for some form of psychological treatment – referred, often, through a long chain of medical practitioners – had been successfully 'treated' once they had been 'discharged' from care, for they rarely represented themselves for further attention. As much as anything, however, this was probably the result of their being absorbed by some other part of the referral chain if they sought further help on subsequent occasions. Working, in more recent years, closer to the community in which they live, I have been struck by how patients, even when they have made very great therapeutic progress, may well re-present themselves for further consultations perhaps on several occasions, but never with quite the same 'problem'. It seems likely that they come back to me because, in contrast with the hospital situation, they know how to find me.

Just as a person whose native language is English may, when living abroad, fall back on it when knowledge of the foreign language is inadequate to meet some particular task or challenge, so the insecure person falls back into the fundamental experience of insecurity whenever events arise to challenge his or her competence in dealing with them. Quite apart from anything else, even the most painful fundamental experiences have the advantage of familiarity. The rejected child at least learns to cope (enough to survive) with rejection, and so may in later life even *seek it out* in preference to an altogether more risky relationship of closeness and confirmation. Better the pain of loneliness than the risk of a new experience of annihilation. One need not have recourse to psychoanalytic jargon ('repetition compulsion') to understand such a process: people deal with the present in terms of the methods and concepts they have learned in the past, and, because of the sheer effort involved if for no other reason, are reluctant to learn new ways. It is as misguided to invoke 'psychopathology' to account for the repetition of 'maladaptive' behaviour as it would be to accuse someone suddenly abducted to China of being mentally ill because, being unable to speak Chinese, they insisted on speaking their native language.

The myth of cure infects our thinking even when we profess to have rejected it, and as one consequence we have an altogether superficial and unsympathetic view of personal change: we overlook the difficulty of change and the pain it demands, as well as the impossibility of eradicating experience. Our view of man is based on objective (largely mechanical) concepts, and we have developed almost no understanding of a subjective psychology appropriate to these issues, even though many of its principles are as obvious as the ground we walk on.

There *are* forms of change which are painless and which may result in such radical improvements in a person's condition that they appear almost to have undergone transformation. But such changes do not come about through the manipulations of doctors or the imprecations of therapeutic gurus: they arise out of changes in the person's *world*. I have known people undergo such radical transformation through events as diverse as being moved to a new council house (which gave a view from its main windows of an open street rather than a smoke-blackened factory wall), learning to drive, and falling in (reciprocated) love. The last of these conditions is perhaps the most common cause of transformation – people who have for years depended on professional help while they struggled with loneliness and despair, may suddenly glow with life, health and optimism if somebody they love falls in love with them. It is certainly something moving and warming to see, even if one trembles a little in anticipation of what may happen as the relationship matures. It is ironic that some research investigators of psychotherapy feel that improvements in patients due to 'significant life events' outside the therapeutic situation should be carefully excluded as cases counting towards success of a particular therapeutic 'technique', for in so doing they exclude the only possible cases which could remotely resemble cure. What strange, mythifying arrogance it is of psychotherapists to feel that they, in the seclusion of their consulting rooms, can undo the ravages which their patients have undergone in their embodied transactions with the world, and that nothing the world does during the course of treatment should be construed as counting towards improvement.

The evils of the world are much too real to be talked away by the myth carriers of our time. And supposing they weren't – what sense could then be made of the struggle of our species to establish itself and its cultures over even those centuries of which we have some knowledge? We are deceived by our magico-religious lust for painless solutions which absolve us from responsibility for our condition into an implicit devaluation of all that is admirable about mankind. For there would be no point in painful struggle, in heroic battle against injustice, in the painstaking achievements of culture and learning, in courageous stance against cruelty or adversity, in loving self-sacrifice for others, if in fact the experience gained by just one tortured and despairing individual could simply be 'adjusted' or 'modified' by the appropriate expert. Our current attitude to suffering would suggest that Jesus Christ could have saved himself a lot of trouble had he had the chance to consult a good psychotherapist.

We are *not* programmable or erasable; our experience of the world is gained through and often at the expense of our living tissue; whether we wish to acknowledge it or not, we are subjects who have wrung a perspective on the world from our embodied experience of it, and our moral evolution, as individuals as well as groups, nations and races, depends upon our making what sense of our experience we can and putting it to the best purpose we can find. There is something about the lessons they draw from their experience of life which human beings are reluctant – indeed, often almost unable – to abandon, and it is senseless of us to praise the courage and integrity of, say, pioneers of science or great moral reformers at the same time as condemning, at least by implication, the views of those who, though equally insistent on the validity of their experience, draw less uplifting conclusions from their knowledge of rejection and brutality; they too may have much more to teach us than we think. It is profoundly, contemptuously disrespectful of individuals for us to characterize the uses to which they put their experience as 'pathological', or to attempt to alter the stance towards the world which they have gained, at great cost, in accordance with some ill-considered professional notion of 'normality'. We can have no clear idea of the shape which moral evolution will take, though we may indeed endeavour to give shape to it, and we need therefore to approach the ways in which other people live their lives with a kind of tentative moral respect if we are not totally to miss the significance of their living at all. Even (indeed, especially) the 'agoraphobic', housebound housewife – the all too familiar patroness of every general practitioner's surgery and psychiatric clinic in the country – constitutes living, embodied testimony to (and protest against) the failures of our social organization; simply to try to 'cure' her, or to talk away her pain, is to dismiss the meaning of her life and to negate her lived moral significance, even though, of course, she herself would be astonished at the idea that her life gave evidence of any such significance. I do not mean to romanticize the life of the 'agoraphobic' – it has no great nobility. But it does have a meaning, it points to a *real* state of affairs, and its pained and distressed aspects cannot be eradicated out of the context which gives rise to them.

Our objectifying language gives us little chance to gain a purchase on the predicaments in which we find ourselves engaged as subjects, so that the experience of distress or anxiety is virtually constrained to take on forms which constitute a kind of language in itself; the expression of our painful relations with the world is to be found in the symbolic aspects of our dread. Whatever the form in which we choose to represent our experience to ourselves, it is inevitably symbolic, just as, of course, language is itself a symbolic medium, and this applies no less to the ways in which our anxiety presents itself to us. Anxiety has a *meaning* which points to a state of affairs in our experience.

Although they seem often absurd, the 'symptoms' of anxiety may actually be speaking a language much more succinct and eloquent than the conventional words we would use to describe the same state of affairs. Moreover (and this is a point to be considered in greater detail towards the end of this book) anxiety as a language may be quite well *understood* even though it cannot be translated into conventional words. However, we should be careful not to mystify the meaning of anxiety by making of it an esoteric symbolism accessible only to those experts initiated into its secrets. The point, rather, is that the way anxiety presents itself is individually meaningful to the person who experiences it, *whether or not* that person can spell the meaning out in conventional language, or, better, *precisely because* he or she cannot.

*John (p. 18), though sensitive to his own and others' feelings, thoughtful and very good at his job as an apprentice joiner, was neither philosophically reflective nor unusually articulate when reviewing his own experience. Even had he been, it is unlikely that he would have found a neater, more economical or accurate metaphor (and it may of course be argued that* all *language is metaphor) for his predicament than that expressed in his fear of falling off the face of the earth. From an objective point of view, of course, this is a crazy idea which makes no apparent sense, though it hit him with the force almost of revelation. For many reasons, I do not believe John could have said to himself, 'I am fearful and uneasy because I have never experienced the confirmation of another person and feel therefore fundamentally insecure, and I live in dread that the few tenuous connexions I have established with others may disintegrate or be snatched away from me. Life seems a terrible risk in this way to me, and I dare not take any kind of step which might jeopardize my fragile security.' All that was a feeling which, very probably, had its origin in the days before he could remember (the days, that is, before he had developed the power of language with which to encode and objectify his experience to himself) and which he experienced as a mysterious dread. A few days before his fear took him over in the middle of the park, he had seen a television documentary which had propounded a number of physical principles, including the law of gravity. Here, suddenly, was a concept which fitted his feeling better than any other he had come across. His disconnectedness and isolation were experienced as if the pull of gravity was about to cease to exist. He experienced his fear as absurd, and kept it a shameful secret for some years. He did not understand his fear in the conventional sense, and yet it carried a conviction for him which he could not ignore. His predicament insisted on recognition in this way, even though the symbolic form taken by this insistence ignored all the rules set by objective discourse; nevertheless, it was more true than anything that discourse had to offer.*

The form taken by 'symptoms' of anxiety is by no means always as neat and eloquent as this, nor as easy to understand. The situation which establishes the subject's painful relation to the world is usually (to the outsider) much more easily identifiable, and probably more important to focus upon, than the symbolic form it takes in the subject's consciousness. In this way, it may well be much more easy to see that Mr Y's fundamental experience of insecurity is leading him to avoid any kind of situation at work which might involve him in angry confrontation with someone in authority than it is to explain why this should present itself symbolically to him in the form of an intense fear of travelling in lifts. The meaning of his fear is clear, but the choice of symbol is less so, though it could probably be found through an investigation of his subjective experience. Not that the fear of lifts need be a *direct* symbol of fear of authority (as may well be assumed by those influenced by the more mechanistic theoretical excesses of psychoanalysis), but rather it is the form seized upon by Mr Y's fear (for what might be quite idiosyncratic reasons) in which to present itself to his consciousness. He (unlike we, who can see much more clearly what he is really afraid of, and why) has to deceive himself about the actual nature of his fear, and, so to speak, look around for something which seems to justify it. 'Phobias' may be of almost anything, from bumblebees to factory chimneys. The point is that they are not absurd, but on the contrary, given the need for self-deception, constitute the best guess (the most sense) the individual can make as to the nature of his predicament, that is, are as near as he can get to a coherent symbolic form or 'description' of his feeling, and satisfy his need for meaning even though they fly in the face of objective factuality.

*Jane (p. 22) would be diagnosed in orthodox psychiatry as suffering from a compulsive-obsessional state, the content of her 'symptoms' being seen (if thought about at all) as a kind of meaningless spin-off from a pathological condition. Her central 'symptom' is a compulsive wish that people she loves should meet with a fatal accident. Particularly with her parents, but sometimes with her children as well, she experiences this wish as popping unbidden into her mind, and she finds it very distressing, feeling both guilty and wicked, and full of a superstitious dread that she might actually have a supernatural power to damage people. It is not difficult to see the significance of this 'symptom': as a child, any kind of negative feeling remotely resembling belligerence or hatred, hostility or rebellion was vetoed, obscured or denied by her parents, who so swamped her with their cloying 'love' that she had scarcely any chance to develop as an individual, own her own feelings or express any independence. Least of all was she able to protest against and attack the 'love' which threatened to destroy her, although she would find herself from time to time doing aggressive things in secret, but without knowing why. But her subjective anger could not be shut out, would not be banished by her verbal denial of it: her 'symptom' was really her telling people to 'drop dead' while she deceived herself that this, though clearly 'a' wish, was not 'her' wish. The possibility for such a self-deception is given by the kind of conceptual structure of our language outlined in the previous chapter: Jane could apparently quite sensibly talk about wishes 'popping into her mind', as if by a faulty electrical circuit, as this is the way we tend to conceptualize wishing, i.e. as a mental act preceding some kind of bodily activity. She was thus permitted not to take responsibility for her anger and hatred even as she gave (though still, of course, in secret) the strongest vent to it.*

'Symptoms' reveal the person's subjective experience of the world, and we fail to read and acknowledge their meaning only because of our desperate need to cling on to the defensive structures of objectivity. 'Symptoms' are as powerful a refutation of myth as one could wish to find.

*Despite her apparently 'successful' life style and all its objective indications of comfort and security, Mary (p. 10) is 'suffering from a depressive illness', as the psychiatrists would say. The very fact that, outwardly, her life is so well ordered and easy seems to point to the 'pathological' nature of her 'condition', and, indeed, she spoke to psychiatrists over many years without one of them ever making any other assumption: not one of them made any kind of serious inquiry into whether her lethargy, her weeping and her despair might indicate* unhappiness. *If, of course, one accepts the objective mythology concerning what is and is not conducive to happiness, then it is clear that Mary* could not be *unhappy, and Mary herself is as convinced a subscriber as anyone to that mythology: she does not believe that her subjective experience can possibly be important enough to contribute to the way she feels. She believes that if the objective circumstances demand that she should be interested, then she should be interested (for example, in the conversation of guests at a party given by her husband for his golf club acquaintances); she believes that if her role as housewife and mother demand cooking and shopping, then she should of course carry out these activities cheerfully and efficiently. In fact, from a very early age, Mary was discouraged from acknowledging and taking account of her own feelings, and, like the other members of her family, was constrained to give precedence to those of her eccentric and demanding father, who, under a cloak of fake but almost frenzied concern, tyrannized all those over whom he had power. The family itself was confused and confusing, and in cluded six children from a collection of marriages, Mary being the youngest and only child of the union then current. At the age of seventeen she had a stormy, unhappy and greatly disapproved-of love affair with a man many years older than herself, and at the end of this married on the rebound a man who seemed to represent the stability, security and confidence she felt she had always wanted. In fact, as she soon discovered (but did not acknowledge), he was a pompous bore who had no interest in women other than as sexual partners, and was afraid of any kind of display of emotion. The marriage declined into a state of guarded coexistence, devoid of warmth and soon enough even of sexuality. Mary deferred to her husband's view that their daughters were best educated in private boarding schools, and did not even 'notice' (i.e., failed to tell herself) how bitterly she missed them. At every point, she regarded the wishes and feelings of others, as she had first learned to do with her father, and disregarded her own. Her subjective, emotional life was a desert, and yet she was simply unable to recognize her own unhappiness. Her 'depression', however, apart from expressing her unhappiness in a manner recognizable at a glance to all those capable of seeing the emperor's nakedness, also provided her with a means of rebellion, for when she was 'ill' she was also prevented form cooking, shopping, and otherwise giving the kind of attention to others which they and she expected of her.*

'Symptoms', then, issue from a subjectivity that will not be gainsaid, and reveal a world which is full of cruelty and pain. Even the 'psychopath', with his 'shallow affect' and his 'incapability of acting in relation to long-term goals' in some ways authentically embodies a statement about the world in which he has lived, for it has been a world in which there *was* no long-term gain, but one in which rewards were few and fleeting, and punishments frequent, violent and brutal; his 'affect' is 'shallow' because he has learned to fake feelings (like love) he has never experienced, and also that to invest emotionally in anything is a risk taken only by mugs.

Our subjective experience of the world tells us the truth about it, even if the language it has to use to do so is cast in forms we have come to see as 'symptoms'. We live in anxiety, fear and dread because these constitute a proper response to the nature of our social world, and if we continue not to take account of the message they give us, we shall make it even more impossible than it has already become to act upon the reality that threatens to imprison and destroy us. So far, however, we have met the challenge of our experience by ever more feverish attempts to objectify ourselves.

# 6 The Magic of the Machine

Several influential thinkers of widely differing persuasions have suggested – in my view convincingly – that it is *in principle* impossible for individual people to give a complete account of their own intentions,* if only because that 'part' of them which is giving the account cannot fall under its own scrutiny: the eye cannot look directly at itself, as it were. As I have already argued, this certainly seems to be the case with people who seek to make sense of their own psychological distress: the conscious (articulate) mythology in terms of which they provide an account of their actions and intentions contrasts strongly with the truer motives which may be inferred from their conduct. Thus their explicit assumptions remain unquestioned until their attention is drawn to the *significance of their conduct.* Their discovery of the falsity of what they had explicitly believed about their intentions is, naturally enough, often attended by pain, confusion, and, at first, almost certainly resistance: one does not willingly or enthusiastically give up beliefs which, however self-deceiving, have protected one from harsh and uncomfortable realizations about the nature of the world and one's own projects in relation to it.

It is my experience, however, that despite its being a relatively unusual idea, individuals do not on the whole have too great difficulty in eventually accepting, at least provisionally, the view that what they say about their motives and intentions has no special claim to accuracy. I have already suggested once or twice that exactly the same state of affairs may obtain at the *collective* level, i.e. in terms of what we tell ourselves as social groups, and even much larger units of organization such as nations and cultures. This, I think, is making much heavier demands on the reader's credulity, since our explicit cultural values (as, for example, the virtues we assume to inhere in science, technology, objectivity, etc.) are strongly reinforced on all sides, and receive the authoritative endorsement of our most respected social institutions. However, it does seem to be the case that with societies as with individuals there is often a striking contrast between our stated aims and the actual results of what we do. Just as the individual's basic assumptions

* I am thinking here of people as contrasting in their approach as, for example, G. Ryle (*The Concept of Mind*, Hutchinson, 1949) and J.-P. Sartre (*Being and Nothingness*, trans. H.E. Barnes, Methuen, 1969).

and projects are almost inevitably buried, uncommented upon, at the centre of his or her conduct, so what we *claim* to be doing collectively may be quite different from the actual achievements of our tacit cultural objectives. We *assume* the rationality of our common activity (necessarily, for if we consciously questioned it, we should presumably be doing something else), and thereafter fail to examine it with any degree of critical detachment, even though our activity may show every indication (as, surely, in many areas of our communal projects it does) of utter irrationality. Though societies of course have their critics, they have nobody much in the role of 'societotherapist', and it is usually only the historian who can provide anything like a convincing account of our true intentions some time after events have revealed what they must have been.

In this chapter, then, I want to suggest a number of quite closely related ways in which, I believe, cultural aims which we take completely for granted contribute to the destructive objectification of individual people and weaken the possibility of their being able to take an effective subjective grasp on the conduct of their own lives and the shaping of their own world. Possibly people may find my observations implausible, or perhaps even offensive; if so, I suggest that this *may* be analogous with the situation in which the individual, faced with a challenge to his or her own version of what he or she is trying to do, will react incredulously or with hostility to the challenger's view. Of course I have absolutely no guarantee that much of what follows may not be the product of an altogether misconceived pessimism, although I find some encouragement in the fact that others who have considered the issues far more thoroughly than I\* have arrived at not dissimilar conclusions.

The need to consider issues at this rather general level arises out of an overemphasis in Western psychology and psychiatry on the part played by *individuals* in the generation of their psychological distress. In fact, the nature of such distress cannot be understood anywhere near fully unless it is placed in the context of our general cultural assumptions and aims, and it is certainly not the case that the processes of objectification which I have tried to identify as lying somewhere near the centre of our malaise are merely the products of individual people who just so happen all to react in rather the same way at this particular point in our development.

\* See, for example, L. Mumford, *The Pentagon of Power*, Harcourt Brace Jovanovich, 1970.

Few of us question that the concepts we find ready and waiting for us on our entry into the social world do anything but reflect an 'obvious' reality. A twentieth-century baby destined to be an astronaut is about to imbibe a cultural world very different from that of a fourteenth-century baby about to become a monk, but, whatever we may think from our supposedly enlightened vantage point, not one which *at the time* carries any more conviction for the individual. With hindsight (and *only* with hindsight) we can criticize aspects of the monk's naturally accepted beliefs, and few would question the sense and value of our doing so. But it takes an act of imagination to criticize our own values and beliefs, and there is, of course, no guarantee that our criticism will be proved justified. However, it is the inevitable lot of human beings, as inescapably *moral* beings, to take that chance, for otherwise our world will not evolve at all, or at least not under our own guidance.

The cultural phenomenon which I particularly want to consider in this chapter, because of its special centrality to the theme of objectification, is that of the cult of the machine. There are several subsidiary reasons for focusing on this particular aspect of present-day existence, most of which, I hope, are also germane to my thesis in one way or another. For example, the machine (at present, in particular, the computer), in representing the most developed extent to which objectification has so far been carried, reveals, I believe, something about our *intentions* towards the world and ourselves. The machine is a ubiquitous feature of our environment, and is accepted as an inevitable (unquestionable) development, even though *in fact*, as a mere product of our activity, its existence could in principle become subject to our conscious control; on the whole, we unhesitatingly endorse the value of progressive mechanization in our explicit consideration of the processes involved, though we fail to take account of what it *actually* does to us and our environment, and express bewilderment and surprise when things turn out to be different from our avowed expectations. We all acknowledge, for example, that many of the fundamental deprivations and injuries suffered by our species could be greatly alleviated if we devoted to them the resources we devote to the refinement of our technological achievements, and we all know that the depletion of our natural resources and the pollution of our world on the scale we at present find necessary to maintain our mechanized way of life cannot be allowed to continue without disaster. And yet we ignore this utterly reasonable assessment of our predicament in favour of a correspondingly *ir*rational belief in the viability of what is in fact a mythical ideal. There are thus, I believe, several parallels between our society in relation to the machine and the individual in relation to his or her personal mythology. The person's mythology forms the very framework through which he or she looks out at the world; our machine culture reflects our values and shapes our experience in ways of which we are unlikely to be aware, and for reasons which are on the whole opaque to us. The largely man-made world which we inhabit did not come about merely by chance, nor by the inexorable unfolding of progress, but by the designs of men and women. These designs, however, are no more conscious and explicit than are the motives of the individual, and if we want to know what they are we must examine the nature of the world around us with a vision which does not simply take everything for granted.

The machine culture, then, does us great damage because it constitutes the mythology which prevents us from getting to grips with what ails us collectively in exactly the same way that the individual's personal mythology prevents him or her from even seeing what features of the world need subjective attention and intervention. Just as the individual in distress will look round for something on which to blame that distress (as, for example, 'illness'), so it is common at the societal level to look round for something, probably a group (capitalists, Marxists, 'extremists') seen as consciously malign, on which to lay the blame for socio-economic breakdown. However, it is usually hard to identify any *actual* malign groups of this kind, just as it is hard to identify the 'illness' thought to be causing the individual's distress. It may be, rather, the *unacknowledged needs and interests* embedded in our social existence, and the defences against their recognition, which cause us trouble, just as it is individuals' unacknowledged aims and strategies which cause them theirs.

Since there are some needs so fundamental that they are shared by all of us, it will scarcely be surprising if we find defences against the vulnerabilities to which they expose us built into the very foundations of our social institutions. If we are not to allow our communal defensiveness to run out of our control, with possibly extremely destructive consequences, we must make strenuous efforts to become aware of (make explicit) the ways in which it dictates our conduct.

Take, for example, the very basic need for *security* which is shared by us all. It is fairly obvious, perhaps, that the initial experience of all those members of our species who survive infancy is likely to be one of *being looked after* when in a state of utter passive dependency. It is therefore not surprising that for the individual *growing up* is an *inevitably* painful process, since built into his or her *bodily experience* is a 'memory' (the knowledge of a feeling) of a time when there was no pain, no frustration or difficulty which could not be solved by a force (in fact, what H.S. Sullivan called 'the mothering one') outside the self, and this 'memory' remains always with us for longing comparison with the painful present in which *nobody* is going to have one's interests that much at heart. All of us therefore know the struggle to escape the pains of maturity and adulthood and the yearning search for dependence on the Other, and we fear also the dangers, indeed terrors, which such dependence implies, since we know that it cannot last. While it may be relatively easy to appreciate the significance of this for the individual, it may be less obvious that we have a *cultural* investment in perpetuating the blissful warmth and safety of the infantile state; even if we can see elements of collective need in, say, 'primitive' religions, we are less ready to see them at work in the revered institutions of our contemporary society.

Again, at the less fundamental level of *interest* (as opposed to need), it is customary in the traditional psychotherapy of so-called 'neurotic' individuals to point to the results of their 'denial' of (i.e. self-deception concerning) their less praiseworthy enterprises, which may for example involve elements of aggression, lust, envy, etc. Collectively, though, we seem less alive to the fact that our self-interest, our economic apprehension and greed, may offer unseen (but much more satisfactory) explanations for our social organization than do the official formulae to which we give quite sincere, if self-deceiving, allegiance. If we do detect such motives, we tend to impute them to some section of society other than that occupied by ourselves.

Thus the pursuit of objectivity, in finding the purest form of its realization in the mechanization of the world and most things in it, including ourselves, serves a number of unstated and unexamined purposes, which include our need for security as well as a number of our less creditable interests.

For example, one of the central security-serving functions of objectivity, in particular as it is embodied in our scientific and technological dogmas, is to relieve us of the painful necessity for making mature, subjective and *ethical* judgments. The ideal world for the kind of 'positivistic' view of science which has dominated the English-speaking intellectual communities in this century is one in which the clarity of 'evidence' and the indisputability of 'facts' obviates the necessity for judging whether one course of action is *better* than another. It is but a short step from here to attempt to realize the removal of the 'human element' of uncertainty and moral choice through the construction of machines (computers) which appear to be concerned solely with the 'facts', and with 'deciding' on the basis of an appraisal of these what is the best course to adopt. To believe in the possibility of any such mechanical solution to our dilemmas is, however, to perform a kind of self-inflicted confidence trick upon ourselves, in which we turn a blind eye to the fact that the computer has been programmed by human beings who have built into it their own human purposes.

Of course there is an essential place for the balanced consideration of matters of fact and of questions of evidence for, and justification of, judgments and propositions, for respect for experience and knowledge and the (as far as possible) disinterested pursuit of truth. It is also the case that the appraisal of facts and the calculation of probabilities can often be carried out very efficiently and quickly by machines (the speed and efficiency with which computers perform what would for people be utterly tedious and laborious tasks – and that is *all* they do – in no way accounts for the awe in which they are held; for that we must seek other explanations). It is clear, however, that none of these laudable operations, however successfully achieved, obviates the necessity for ethical judgment and moral concern, and the exercise of these faculties can, *in principle*, never be detached from human beings, nor ever escaped by them. It is a philosophical truism that however much is known about the factual aspects of any particular issue, it is still always possible to ask whether it is *right*, and to that *ethical* question there can be no certain answer, no deliverance from the necessity of making a fallible human judgment. A child, certainly, may leave the exercise of such judgment to its parents, but for the adult there is no such escape.

The cult of objectivity, in trying to make us secure from the necessity for taking account of the subjective, ethical aspects of our intellectual and social culture, simply becomes blind to their actual influence, which then runs out of control giving unchecked *moral* fervour to our pursuit of the objective, and making it impossible for us to identify what *particular* moral concern might be lurking behind so-called 'value-free' objective investigations and 'factual' pronouncements. On the one hand this kind of approach embodies a fervent hope which, however attractive, is really as obviously and as absurdly naive as any belief in witchcraft, and on the other it sets up a kind of inverted moralism* of its own which views any kind of assertion of subjective or ethical values with (in 'non-factual' areas) contempt or derision, or (in areas which could be regarded as 'factual') deep hostility and disapproval.

One effect of this, as far as the man-in-the-street is concerned, is to make personal judgments about the desirability or otherwise of states of affairs or courses of action something which he can no longer see as his prerogative, if indeed he does not see them as actually reprehensible. You have no right to a view if you 'don't know the facts', and to expound one is impudently to usurp the function of 'experts', or even more reliable machines, from which, so it seems, every last possibility of error has been removed. Not only do 'ordinary people' feel they have no right to comment on 'things they don't understand', but, particularly significantly for the focus of this book, they come to feel incapable of judging even the significance and sanity of their own conduct.

Thus, in our society, balanced judgment, knowledge of facts, 'scientific' and technical expertise become the property of an elite class of professionals, who alone are seen as being in a position to judge the uses to which such knowledge should be put. Subjective, ethical judgment and conduct become inverted and out of sight. This then leaves the 'ordinary person' with very little role at all, except as object and consumer, for he or she has neither the 'training' nor the 'expertise' to make balanced, objective judgments, and depends utterly on the professionals – academics, scientists, medics, lawyers, technicians, etc. – for the exercise of these capacities. Thus a faith in objectivity which serves to preserve our security also comes to serve the interests of those who become its conceptual custodians. It is not that the experts maintain their monopoly with any conscious malice or greed – in fact most would feel as well as profess a pride in their reputation for probity and a genuine satisfaction in their service to others. It needs a painful effort of 'consciousness-raising' even to begin to see what, for example,

* The concept of 'moral inversion' was developed first by M. Polanyi in his book *Personal Knowledge*, Routledge and Kegan Paul, 1958.

Ivan Illich means when he writes about the 'disabling professions'.* To take the most severe view, however, it is possible to see professional experts as being on the one hand like intellectual usurers who, as it were, hire out their concepts to the uninitiated, and on the other hand like a priesthood which mediates the mysteries of objective knowledge to the masses, but does not permit them entry to them.

To pursue for a moment the first of these analogies, it certainly seems that a large part of the *actual activity* of professional academics, scientists, etc., is aimed at keeping their knowledge as a kind of intellectual capital which may be employed to make money at interest without itself becoming dissipated into the beliefs, practices and preoccupations of ordinary people – hence perhaps the enormous energy put quite overtly by professional groups in these fields into protecting their rights and claims to exclusive knowledge and competence, etc. The economic basis of production and consumption in which we are all, willy nilly, caught up, is thus reflected in the structure and functions of our scientific and intellectual institutions. Psychotherapy, for example, is as much an industry as is steel manufacture or entertainment; universities have in many fundamental respects become factories for the production of 'knowledge' the primary function of which is to perpetuate the academic industry itself by manufacturing the raw material which keeps it going. If this latter seems a harsh judgment, one need only reflect that both teachers and students in universities are in their own (not consciously perceived) interest forced to act (produce) *like* teachers and students if they are to justify their continued existence in an overcrowded and competitive academic world. It is obvious that in these circumstances mere quantity of output will become more important than quality of work (it is also, let it be noted, more easily objectively measurable). Thus I have seen academic boards set up for senior university appointments make preferences for one candidate rather than another on the basis of the *number* of publications listed in the candidate's curriculum vitae, *without any attempt being made* to consider the content or intellectual quality of the publications. Similarly, considerable debate has taken place in the pages of the main professional journal of British psychologists (*The Bulletin of the British Psychological Society*) seriously advocating the measurement of psychologists' academic worth

---

* I. Illich *et al., Disabling Professions,* Marion Boyars, 1977.

by the *number* of publications they produce. The parallels of this kind of approach with industrial production seem to me inescapable, as does its irrelevance to anything one might naively have associated with academic excellence. Again, students have complained to me that their teachers, though sometimes representing extremely opposed intellectual positions, will not confront each other in public over their differences, but instead advocate a kind of tolerant eclecticism in which the concept of truth quietly disappears. This seems hard to understand as anything but a function of the setting in which teachers depend heavily for their academic advancement on winning research grants from both public and private bodies, so that they *cannot afford* to be wrong, and hence unconsciously suppress public disagreement amongst themselves, as well as the opportunity for outsiders to criticize their activities. This is highly understandable (which of us would not do the same?) but nevertheless militates against traditional (possibly even mythical?) values of intellectual honesty and debate, and at the same time subtly appropriates knowledge as the *production* of a particular professional group.

That self-interest and greed play a large part (albeit unconsciously) in these processes, as indeed they do so obviously in our more overtly economic institutions, is perhaps easy enough to see. What may less readily be appreciated is the extent to which the general population becomes intellectually subjugated thereby. One result of this is the enormous gullibility and unreflectiveness of the 'ordinary' person in matters which have become professional property. For example, laymen's expectations of science and medicine are almost boundlessly naive (and their surprise when confronted personally with medical and scientific failures correspondingly exaggerated) since they have, in a sense, given up their right to consider or criticize. Consideration and criticism have become part of the *professional's* special prerogatives; for laymen, theirs is only to wonder and consume.

Lurking behind the sheer economic self-interest of intellectual and technical professionalization is, I believe, an inverted form of the moral zeal which once fuelled our religions. The science-based professions are not simply cynically out to feather their own nests and make monkeys of those to whom they sell their services. More fundamentally, they are gripped, like the rest of us, by a dream of how the world might be, and inflated with a sense of their own mission in bringing it about.

Just as the priest interprets to the laity a reassuring vision of love and redemption, or at least the possibility of salvation, so the scientist conveys to the lay populace the possibility of a world in which all 'problems' are soluble, all need for subjective judgment potentially redundant, all pain and despair in principle curable. Like the priest, the scientist expounds these mysteries in terms incomprehensible to the layman, but socially authorized and hence believed. Our attitude to scientific and technical matters is soaked through with awe, and the uninitiated will drink in the banalities and fake profundities of, say, televisual scientific acolytes with a credulity quite as blind as that of any newly converted religious zealot.

'Scientists think . . .' and 'scientists have shown . . .', etc., form the preamble to countless statements of almost infinite implausibility, to which, because of their apparent scientific legitimation, the layman is expected to give immediate credence. This, moreover, is not simply the result of a popular corruption of matters surpassing lay understanding, but a clear reflection of attitudes held by many scientists themselves. At least in the social sciences (I have no first-hand experience of others) it is common for practitioners and theoreticians to spend considerable amounts of time and energy in admitting or excommunicating fellow members to or from the scientific club on the grounds of whether or not their work conforms to *dogmatic* rules concerning what it is to be 'scientific'. For the most part, these are the rules of objectivity and mechanism, and bear only the most distant relationship to questions of importance, interest, or truth.

It seems to me fairly obvious that at least in part science had its origin in a reaction *against* a view of knowledge as dogmatic or established by authority, insisting instead that personal experience, or at least those aspects of it which can be shared with others, provide the grounds upon which claims about the nature of the world can be made. This enormously liberating position almost immediately (as seems so often to be the way with great moral or philosophical insights) became itself ossified into a dogmatic orthodoxy which by now holds sway in our intellectual institutions with an almost unassailable repressive force. Just as a religion may become obsessed with its forms and its rituals to the complete neglect of its moral content, so science has become utterly preoccupied with its methods (for example, objectification, quantification, mechanization) and almost indifferent to the content to which its methodology is applied. For example, it is far more important for a Ph.D. student of psychology to employ the officially approved methods of measurement and experimental design than it is for him or her to apply them to any particularly interesting issue or question. In part, no doubt, this is because interesting questions, seriously addressed, would not provide enough raw material to support a large academic industry, but it is also true that recitation of the dogmatic scientific creed is a virtually necessary act for admission to a priesthood dedicated to upholding the values of objectification. This again is, I believe, a largely unconscious process (in the sense of not being explicit or avowed): it is not the case that those who embody 'the system' – e.g. academic teachers of psychology – see themselves as guardians of a repressive orthodoxy. I am sure they would be appalled at any such suggestion. Rather is it the case that this is the result of their conduct, whatever they may claim to be doing.

As with the self-deceptive manoeuvres by which individuals attempt to defend themselves from painful recognition of their predicament, so the culturally embedded defences of objectivity frequently defeat the very aim which they profess to be pursuing. While the explicit aim may be an altogether laudable one of furthering a commonly acknowledged cultural value, the implicit one (judged by what in fact we manage to achieve in our cultural institutions) may well be once again to prevent us from catching a glimpse of our own vulnerability. For example, medicine, and too often nursing, rather than cultivating the arts of tenderness and concern, may tend to foster a kind of stony indifference to the emotional vulnerability of those they 'care' for (there is no institution less comforting than the 'traditional' hospital). Our school system, in its obsession with 'techniques' of teaching and the relatively narrow definition of curricula, becomes blind to the complexity of the processes and content of learning, so that while a school may indeed be a most potent source of learning for children (e.g. in terms of what they learn about each other), *what* is learned may have almost nothing to do with the official curriculum, and what is learned outside school hours, because it falls under no official or objective demarcation of 'training', is unlikely to be conceived of as learning at all. The way in which learning actually does take place is likely to be very different from 'official' views concerning the 'acquisition of skills', etc. I have already suggested ways in which the achievements of some of our institutions of higher education may depart from those traditionally associated with them. All in all we pay a heavy price for the reassurance we gain from the conviction that the automatic progress of science and technology will ensure a satisfactory future while removing from us the necessity for personal, subjective judgment or intervention in the world's affairs, since we alienate from ourselves our ability to determine the quality of our social existence.

Almost the only visible shred left of anything approaching moral concern in the actual conduct of our official institutions has come to be couched in (objectively measurable) financial terms. For example, it is taken as *self-evident* by many National Health Service psychologists (whom I single out only because I know them best) that 'cost effectiveness' should be their primary consideration when evaluating the 'treatments' they apply. To question whether what is good for patients must *necessarily* be connected with what is relatively less expensive is to be regarded with slightly disapproving non-comprehension. Literally not to count the cost of what one does for patients is to invite *moral* disapproval. Money thus becomes an objective substitute for more subjective qualities like concern, interest or care. (This is not, of course, to suggest that financial questions are *irrelevant* to the provision of services.)

And yet this investment in an apparently cool practicality, this hard-headed invocation of objective and 'scientific' standards, is in truth only a mask for a form of idealism which, if it continues to go unchecked and unnoticed, threatens to degenerate into an uncontrolled yearning for a magical state of freedom from pain and threat, in which human beings become the invulnerable and immortal foetuses of an enormous, impersonal, technological womb. The longings and illusions we once hoped to realize through religion we now see, through a kind of greedy haze of mounting excitement, as being obtainable – thanks to 'science' – here on earth. Through the use of drugs, and spare parts, processes of conditioning or hypnosis, the ever more 'miraculous' discoveries and promises of science, our fantasies of everlasting life, unmitigated ease and plenty, seem tantalizingly to approach ever closer to our grasp. And in pursuit of this we abandon our subjectivity, and retreat from our reason.

So blind is our faith that objectivity will deliver us from evil, that we become incapable of seeing the evil around us; so much more vivid are our dreams than our perception of reality that we can only gaze fondly upon them as, unconsciously, we embark upon the destruction of our world. Soberly we contemplate the Frankensteinian reveries of 'scientists' who speculate with barely suppressed excitement about the implications of 'breakthroughs' which offer to halt the processes of ageing, restore or erase memories, activate 'pleasure centres' in our brains, and in other ways spare us the boring necessity of actually having to deal with the world. Mouths agape like the dupe of Bosch's mediaeval conjuror, we credit these and other self-deceiving illusions with infinite plausibility just as long as they are offered to us by our accredited scientific priests, never once pausing to reflect that, for example, our experience of the world depends on more than the mere mechanical processes of our bodies, and that if we were to succeed in encapsulating ourselves off from the world outside our skins, ceasing to take responsibility for what we do to it, we should simply be destroyed. Tinkering, however 'scientifically', with our minds and our bodies will never make the *world* a better place.

The solemn surprise with which we point to the 'prescience' of futurist writers like H.G. Wells, the naivety of our ponderous astonishment at the coming to pass of the erstwhile fantasies of science fiction, are surely pointers to the extent to which we have blinded ourselves to the nature of our own undertakings. Sublimely unaware that our science and our science fiction are but aspects of the *same* subjective impulse, the latter providing the blueprint for the former, we act as if those who first give words to our imaginings somehow 'foresee' the awe-inspiring achievements of 'objective' developments which come about apparently untouched by human minds. The vast mechanical world which we have created is, of course, not the inevitable achievement of a value-free science and technology, the necessary result of the unlocking of nature's secrets, but rather the concrete realization of our seemingly relentless urge to achieve our wildest dreams. (This fusion of the objective with the religious, hard fact with wild fantasy, dry mathematical efficiency with a kind of half-conscious, slightly decadent lack of moral restraint, seems often to be found in science fiction, and may go some way towards accounting for its often compulsive quality, and for the slightly dazed and sickened feeling with which one surfaces from it!)

Naturally, we take for granted our attitude to our own technological achievements, and yet, if something like the analysis offered here is not correct, *some* explanation has to be found for our fusion of the scientific with the magical and religious. Why else, for example, do we so often speak of the 'wonders' of modern science, the 'miracles' of medicine; what explains our awed fascination with technical developments and electronic machines? After all, such achievements are in fact extremely prosaic, absolutely explainable and understandable (since we have constructed them ourselves) down to the last detail. It must be, I think, that we infuse them with the wordless longings of our infancy, and with inarticulate religious hope. (The very day following the writing of these words, a television programme describes in one breathless sentence an American clinic for plastic surgery (!) as: 'A *Mecca* to which *pilgrims* trek who are seeking medical *miracles*'.) Through a kind of generalized Myth of the Machine, into which we project all our unacknowledged craving for comfort and security, we seem to have found a way of actually constructing for ourselves the God in whom our hopes had begun to founder.

There seems little doubt that most people are only too happy to conceptualize themselves in mechanical terms – the most recent fashion in academic psychology, for example, is to develop theoretical understandings of 'human behaviour' from analogies based on the workings of computers. Almost no attempt to understand human nature in 'scientific' terms has paid serious attention to man's subjectivity and essentially moral nature – indeed to do so would (ludicrously, in my view) in itself be considered 'unscientific'. The 'computer model' is but the latest in a long line of mechanical analogies in psychology, earlier versions of which (like Freud's) based themselves on concepts more appropriate to hydraulics or steam engines. Today, as before, any attempt to understand human nature through even a commonsense appraisal of people's *experience* of their world is rejected in favour of theoretical positions which invoke psycho-biological mechanisms of one kind or another. On the one hand this kind of approach leads to a gross distortion of the meaning of our experience; on the other it specifies the conceptual moulds into which we have to fit ourselves and thus determines the limits within which we are able to understand ourselves. The more we feed the mechanistic myths which govern our thinking about ourselves – the more, that is, we appear to have an acceptably 'scientific' understanding of our nature – the more, in fact, we become unable to acknowledge, interpret, or talk about our own experience.

For example, because we treat sex as largely a mechanical 'drive', placing great emphasis on its 'optimal' functioning and being constantly vigilant for breakdowns or 'dysfunctions' in the sexual machinery, we pay virtually no attention to people's *actual experience* of their sexuality. We find it more important to preserve and foster the myth of sexuality as mechanical process than we do to develop any kind of detailed or sensitive phenomenology of sexual experience (i.e., establishing how *in fact* people experience their sexual needs and feelings). I suspect that a vast proportion of people live in secret unhappiness about their sexuality because they are unable to meet what are in truth entirely mythical 'norms' of 'performance'. In this context, for example, I am struck by how many women seem to find sex a less impelling need after some period of married life, usually after the birth of their children, and how they endeavour to disguise this fact from their husbands, who they rightly suspect will wrongly interpret their lack of sexual interest as lack of love. Aspects of this situation are of course far from unnoticed in our culture, and indeed are a reliable source of comic material, but I know of no 'official' movement to take what people feel seriously enough to suggest that an open appraisal and discussion of what seems to be a common experience might ease some of the tensions which so often lead to marital disaster in middle life. Rather, women who feel this way may guiltily conceal what they fear to be 'sexual dysfunction' while men continue to be haunted by fantasies of what a 'real woman' would be like. As one of the primary 'drives' fuelling the entire mechanical process which life has become, sex develops into an increasingly undifferentiated, urgent preoccupation, a kind of life-long, meaningless lust, ready to be tended and if necessary stoked by a horde of experts if it shows any signs of flagging.

If, however, we were prepared to examine the meaning of people's sexual experience, to acknowledge the fluctuations and changes it undergoes at various times in our lives, the differing experiences of men and women in relation to their sexuality, we might not only learn to feel more comfortable with ourselves and each other, but sex itself might become a slightly less prominent cultural obsession, and take its place alongside other important human preoccupations. This, of course, is speculation based on my experience of being able to talk to people about their sexual feelings with a degree of honesty. It would be foolish of me to claim on this basis any kind of expertise on sexual matters, but it does prompt me to wonder what we might be able to know about ourselves if we were not constrained to see ourselves as machines: if, that is, we could talk about our experience rather than our myths.

Because the Myth of the Machine has gained such sway over our outlook, we can only think in terms of things 'working' in a well oiled, predictable, comfortable way. We cannot easily conceive, for example, of life being *necessarily* painful: if we are not 'happy', something must have 'gone wrong'. I suspect, for instance, that the occurrence of so-called 'depressive illness' among the middle-aged and elderly (the 'endogenous depression' particularly likely to be regarded by psychiatrists and others as physically caused disease) is especially poorly understood because of our failure to pay serious attention to our experience and to develop a language in which it can be discussed. Gradually to become old can for many people be a particularly painful experience, and one for which life, however well ordered, 'successful', etc., offers little compensation. The loss of one's children, one's influence and social and economic status, the decline in one's physical and mental powers, the ever more certain knowledge of approaching death, the experience of the death of others, are, to be sure, part of a natural and 'normal' process and cannot therefore reasonably be complained about without placing an unfair strain on those around one. And yet to glimpse these factors – which can scarcely be ignored for long – in a world in which all the explicit emphasis is on ease and pleasure, happiness, youth, sex and 'success', in which the ideal is to be passively nurtured in a giant mechanical womb, is to find oneself in an almost unthinkably lonely and frightening condition which one is simply not prepared to face. Thus our ability to confront, acknowledge and come to terms with this *inevitably* painful state of affairs is seriously depleted, so that almost the only possibility open to us is to slide into a kind of numb 'depressive illness' which will give us licence to be stunned by drugs or electricity into a state of relative indifference to our circumstances and our future.

*John (pp. 18, 94) has not complained of any of his 'symptoms' for over a year, but on this occasion keeps returning to the feeling of dizziness and nausea which has been troubling him for the past few weeks. He says he cannot understand it, is worried that it might be something serious, and though willing superficially to accept the idea that it is just a touch of tension, shows no interest in talking about anything else. He looks ill at ease, and his insistent focusing on 'symptoms' becomes quite*

*irritating to the therapist. John cannot identify anything that is
troubling him – 'things are all right, nothing's wrong'. Only
when the therapist, on a hunch, asks him how his daughter is
does the truth begin to emerge. 'They don't seem to need you so
much, do they?' says John, and goes on to talk about how his
daughter, now fifteen, is going out more without him and acting
more often on her own initiative rather than seeking his advice.
Hobbies which they had shared she now pursues quite often on
her own, and she tells him less about the events of her life. It has
always been clear that she is the apple of John's eye, and he has
been an involved, but lovingly encouraging and non-intrusive
parent. His expression is full of a kind of diffident pain as he
describes his daughter's growing up. 'For a moment', he says,
'you wonder if you've done something wrong, don't you?' He and
the therapist then discuss issues to do with the intense sadness
which a parent may feel over a child's growing up, and as a
result, it seems, John is able to integrate and accept a feeling
which until then had just been an unexplained physical nausea;
he feels able to feel his feelings and accept himself as normal.
(I know of no psychiatric or psychological text which acknowledges such feelings as real, profound, in a sense 'incurable'
sources of pain, i.e. as legitimate causes of distress. It is therefore no wonder that people misinterpret their feelings as 'symptoms' and cannot for themselves find the words to describe
them.)*

A sensitive, subjective appraisal of the world in which we
live, as well as of our own nature, uncovers misery which
cannot be escaped, risks which cannot be sidestepped. As we
struggle to avert our gaze from these, they become, in the
corner of our eye, terrors which must be avoided at all costs,
and so we construct our semi-magical machine world which
promises to ward off evil for ever. To fit into this machine world
we must also make machines of ourselves, and we do so with
enthusiasm. We become plastic, standardized, passive con-
sumers, intent upon deadening our own unease. Patients who
for one reason or another have perforce stumbled across their
subjectivity are apt tremulously to ask 'are there other people
like me?', as if the experience of pain, fear or doubt is about to
place them outside the bounds of humanity, as if the only safe
way of 'being' is as one of millions of identical units all of whom
act and feel similarly and predictably. Every secondary school
child knows that to be 'different' is to invite suspicion, hostility

and ridicule; the Other's eye is naturally drawn to the conspicuous (the feeling of conspicuousness is often the most salient
component in the experience of 'phobic' anxiety). The attraction
of machine status, of serfdom in its modern form, is protection
from an unkind world and from the Other who strikes you
down if you dare to become a person; and so we invent a
mythified 'force' of impersonal objectivity (invested in 'science'
or 'progress') which promises to look after our interests far
more reliably and impartially than any Jehovah could have
managed.

There is one particular mechanical medium – television –
which shapes the nature of our reality more than almost any
other, though most of us, I suspect, hardly notice the pervasiveness of its influence since it has become such an established
part of our experience. In fact, television is the near-perfect
expression of our self-deceiving urge to take our mythology for
the truth. Its greatest asset in this respect is its plausibility:
seeing is believing, the camera cannot lie. And yet, in so cred-
ibly putting before us the world in which we wish to believe,
it distorts and betrays just about every truth and value of
the non-magical, non-mechanical world in which, unless we
actually do turn into machines, we are still constrained to live.
Television pacifies, deludes and bemuses us to such an extent
that we can scarcely even look at the real world without wanting
to adjust its contrast and colour balance (looking at some slightly
purple coloured fields not long ago, I found myself actually
thinking that something must be wrong with the colour control).

Television fulfils our wildest magical dreams while appearing
to present us with reality. Everything which offends our
mythology can be laundered out of what is presented to us
through the process of editing: the aged and ugly, the sick and
deformed will not be invited to appear as contestants on the
quiz shows; the unscripted outburst can be cut out of the
recording, the camera pick and choose what it wants us to see.
The relatively unbounded money and power available to television production, combined with its technical possibilities,
mean that we are bombarded with magical images – ordinary
people can be transported from their ordinary world and find
themselves suddenly confronting their relatives in Australia,
being flown to New York, or presented after fifty minutes of
inane entertainment with a shining new car which is driven
into the very room where they stand by a girl in a bikini.

If asked, of course, we would claim to have 'insight' into our addiction to this cultural diet, would claim to know that it is 'only entertainment'. But this is as self-deceiving as saying that one knows one's 'symptoms' (of psychological distress) are 'silly', for what we fail properly to notice and take account of is that we are indeed addicted, and that there must be reasons for it. Why, for example, does so much highly expensive 'peak viewing time' get spent on presenting to us the odd and the quirky: astrologers who foretell the lives of royal babies, eccentric ladies who feel that they can communicate with their cats, vicars who imitate the sounds made by railway trains? Could it not be because these and others like them have their own special place in constructing for us a kind of comfortably whimsical world in which we like to believe (continuous perhaps with the fairytale world we like to create for our children)?

Television is not, however, particularly concerned not to offend our traditional moral values (it is our *mythology* it preserves at all costs): the endless stimulation of voyeuristic sexual interest, prurience and violence (epitomized in the official speculation that, with the advent of cable television, shift workers could have the benefit of one or two channels of non-stop pornography) testify to the fact that television's is not a *conventional* moral concern. The tacit aim of television, rather, is to keep us from catching a glimpse of the world in which we actually live, the world in which real pain, real love, actual death, loss and despair, real struggle and conflict, economic and social deprivation play such a prominent part. Instead, television feeds our passive torpor by permitting us to sink into the semi-conscious world of our most primitive dreams and fantasies, in which we may indulge the half-formed urges for personal, tribal and sexual conquest which slosh about in the sumps of our minds. Any visiting Martian anthropologist intent on gauging our values from the way we spend our spare time would surely be appalled at what television reveals as our major preoccupations.

Time and space are, in television, also given distorted, magical dimensions, the unspoken aim of which seems to be to insulate us from, and eventually blunt, our natural emotional reactions. Images of corpses crawling with flies will be followed in a flash by one of an old lady winning the football pools. Hardly has one had time to focus one's eyes on a scene in which desperate citizens are being bludgeoned by riot police when the image is replaced by that of the arrival at some airport of an international superstar dressed in a glittering suit. We may be reassured that none of this is real because it flits across our consciousness so rapidly that we have no time to digest its significance before our emotions are jerked away and engaged in some quite different sphere. With a kind of convoluted hypocrisy, television can even remove from us the responsibility for looking at what it shows us – I remember a news reporter, even as the cameras dwelt on the tattered remnants of people and their personal effects at the scene of an appalling air crash, berating in tones of the highest moral indignation those 'ghouls' who had driven out to inspect the event for themselves.

The exigencies of programme timing mean that no issue, however complex or interesting, can be aired beyond its allotted span. In fact, this means that complexity and interest become extinct qualities: the pundits and personalities, the 'experts' who will be invited and reinvited to present their views, are those for whom interest, profundity, scholarship, moral sensibility and complexity can be sacrificed to 'image'. The real people may only be glimpsed occasionally, and then by mistake, but the images we see are of instant people with instant ideas and instant reactions to the imperious demands of television technology; they bear as much relation to real people as instant potatoes do to real potatoes. Our mythical world demands blandness in all things, easy solutions, the ability to flit as fast as light from the potentially painful to the reassuring.

Television feeds our passivity through its ability to remove from us the need for patience and attentiveness. Because of the technical possibilities offered by editing, 'replays', etc., the actual texture of experience is altered, both on and off the screen. For example, sporting events become 'action-packed' series of incidents, and real, non-televisual sport has to be changed – simplified, made more 'spectacular', less 'boring', more instantly consumable – in order to accord with the expectations generated in both spectators and players by television. Again, we approach in this way the binary, all or nothing world of the computer, in which there is no time for subtlety, patience or ambiguity.

Attending to detail, effortfully trying to understand, is an active process, and like all active processes relatively painful. Attention to content, to detail, is in television sacrificed to fascination with style. Politics becomes a gladiatorial spectacle in which the struggle for power or the occurrence of 'splits' absorbs all the interest which might otherwise be invested in how and for what that power might be used. What people have to say becomes far less important than how they say it. Partly to preserve us from the 'heaviness' of their subject matter, and partly perhaps to enhance their status as magicians, the pundits must display strange gestures, quirky mannerisms or funny voices if they are to be able to 'explain' to us the mysteries of botany, or astronomy, or 'science' is general. There is no place on the television screen for the serious and the concerned (unless it is mock seriousness and concern) for these are the kind of qualities of spontaneous subjectivity which demand hesitant, often ambiguous complexity. The fabricated personae of television 'people' are the necessary outcome of the posed self-consciousness which the medium demands, and yet for most of us these are the 'people' we 'know' best, the acquaintances we have in common with millions (this, of course, gives a quite bogus, simplified structure to our socal existence, distracting us from the painful complexity of our relations with real people who, in comparison, are likely to be enigmas to us).

The pace of 'serious' programmes is, in terms of what we are asked to digest, extremely easy. Again, the lumps are ironed out, the contentious issues ignored. Even with the aid of a video recorder, you cannot easily flick back and forth through the material (as you can with a book), so that the effort has to be taken out of understanding through repetition and over-simplification, and your being offered nothing which demands questioning or reflection. The television viewer exists in a world which is complete and finished, ready to be transmitted in easy stages. He or she is there to consume the world, not to create it.

Because we may consider the camera lens as objective and impartial, we may feel it scarcely rational to entertain the idea that television embodies values of its own (ultimately, of course, these are the values with which our split-off and denied – inverted – subjectivity has invested it). Television imposes, certainly, its own unwritten etiquette, and its unstated but almost absolute power to determine our reality leads to a quite general and apparently unquestioning acceptance of its manners. Central to these is precisely television's implicit claim to objectivity, so that the interviewer, who, largely unseen, becomes the camera's voice, is enabled to ask questions which would in any other context be considered offensive, impertinent, or stupid. But, so it seems, his (or hers) is the voice of objective inquiry, and may not itself be questioned. The objects of such inquiry, transfixed by both camera and voice, thrown perhaps suddenly into the bright arena of 'real' reality (as against the shoddy world of everyday life), stutter and stammer and search their verbal repertoire for any kind of idiocy or irrelevance rather than fail to answer, or ask a question of their own. The camera, in other words, exacts the instant and willing abandonment of the person's last shred of subjectivity. The grief-stricken widow will actually pause in her weeping to tell the voice 'how she feels'; the cornered politician will overlook the hectoring moralism of the voice in order to try to justify a position which, between them, the voice and the camera have already rendered untenable. Association with a television camera seems to justify almost any kind of intrusion. Occasionally, presumably, a person may rebel against the insolent impositions of the camera-voice (by asking it a question, for example), but if so, no doubt this evidence of subjective power will be edited from the tape before it gets a chance to subvert us.

The passivity of the person in relation to television is expressed in almost beautiful symbolism by the development of cable television. Like a great umbilical cord, the cable snakes to your set from some huge central placenta, promising to relieve you of the necessity for activity, creativity, thought, or even, eventually, movement. Passive consumption as opposed to active involvement is already the keynote of pre-cable television, but the multiplicity of channels offered by the cable means that you can be almost infinitely capricious with the choice of your diet if too heavy demands are made on your digestion. And even literally, once the potential for 'information technology' has been realized through your cable, you will not have to move from your sofa to order your breakfast.

Television's is the world of the 'image', and the camera constitutes the eye of the Other which renders self-conscious all those who become aware of its gaze. Television's ability to turn us into objects – to realize, that is, one of our most profound magical wishes – may go some way to explaining our readiness to accord *its* world a fundamental reality and to accept the necessity it imposes upon us to make the world of our experience fit in with its technical constraints and demands. People will distort the natural space-time of their experience in order to accommodate the needs of television – even 'spontaneous' expressions of joy or sorrow may be delayed until the cameras arrive on the scene. The dimensions in which ordinary activities take place, the timing of celebrations (as in pre-recorded 'Christmas' shows), the appropriateness of human conduct (as when junior school children are taught – no doubt as part of a 'training' in 'media skills' – to smile at cameras or talk to 'people' they will never meet) may all be altered to conform to what once might have seemed the *limitations* of television technology. But those limitations now come to be accepted as the prestigious accoutrements of a manufactured reality which promises to provide us with objective being. We are ready, it seems, to trade in the natural world of our experience, to sacrifice spontaneity and unreflective absorption with each other and the world, for a self-consciously fabricated image of how we should like things to be. In doing this we have failed to notice the quite untrammelled licence we have given to our magico-religious dream of escaping from our subjectivity. We smile indulgently at those 'primitive' peoples who refuse to be photographed for fear of losing their souls, when in fact we might envy their still having souls to lose. As for us, we become the mechanical terminals of the machines we have created.

Indeed, it is hard now to believe that in many ways we have not actually achieved the state of affairs in which the machines control us rather than we them. Quite apart from television, which hynotically draws people out of interaction with each other, there seem to be endless ways in which we become plugged into machines which render us oblivious to our human surroundings. It is scarely possible any longer to find a pub in which conversation is not drowned out by the juke box, the electronic explosions of the space invaders and the bleeping of the fruit machines. Like automata ourselves, we stand in front of these machines, the movements of our eyes and limbs stereotyped and repetitive, controlled by a mechanical program which determines precisely the limits of our freedom. Already quite possibly slightly deafened by discos, young people walk or cycle down the street with headphones clamped to their ears ('wired for sound', in the words of a pop song), cut off from any possibility of mutual relationship with their world. Girls in offices sit with docile attentiveness before the balefully glowing green screens of computer terminals and word processors which type fake 'personal' letters to potential customers whose names have been swallowed up into the software (no 'neurotic' dislocation of words from reality could be more poignant than the way in which we have learned to speak about the 'personalized' communications of computers).

Almost every human ability and characteristic which can be mechanized has been siphoned off from our subjectivity and translated into plastic and electronic circuitry. And we, enslaved to the machines, passively consume from them the fruits of the very abilities of which they have robbed us – more accurately, of which we have robbed ourselves and built into them. With our willing connivance, the machines, and of course the professionals and experts whose interest it is to tend them, have taken over and objectified the subjectivity of 'ordinary people', who become emptied-out objects unable to reintegrate what is rightfully theirs, but who can, for a price, effortlessly consume what once they might have been able effortfully to create. No longer needing, for example, to make music, people can surround themselves with stacks of stereophonic gadgetry from which they can hear music as digitally faultless as technology can make it. 'Entertainment', as well as 'communication', have become the prerogatives of a tiny minority of professional experts (the globally familiar celebrities and pundits) whose already highly practised abilities are electronically perfected and offered for mass consumption to us, the public, who no longer see music, art, discussion or even thought as any part of our own 'skills', and who, as unprotestingly as battery chickens (themselves, let it be noted, animals we have mechanized), accept an ever more narrowly standardized cultural diet fed to us through our brushed aluminium hoppers.

In this way we become mere shells, passively consuming via a highly evolved technology an artificial world which is increasingly insulated from any effort we might make to impinge upon it. This is not the result of the evil machinations of any particular group or class (though clearly some people's interests will be served by this state of affairs more than others'), but rather the upshot of a magic-infused mythology in which to a greater or lesser extent we all collude, and which may well have its roots in the greedy passivity we all experience as infants.

Since, however, the real world continues to exist, we find ourselves from time to time rudely awakened from our wishful dreams to confront issues which cause us unexpected and incomprehensible pain. Far from being an indication of our own malfunctioning, this may yet provide us with the spur we need to recognize and confront the reality of the world, to accept responsibility for the mechanized impoverishment of our lives, and to reassert our subjectivity. But, predictably, our first impulse is to look for technical solutions to our troubled dreams.

# 7   The Experts

When the myth-infused structures which support the objectified individual's sense of security split open to reveal the
threats of the real world, he or she is likely to interpret this as a
form of mechanical breakdown. In this chapter I want to consider – necessarily only in outline – those forms of professional
help which are most widely available to those who seek it when
they feel in need of a degree of repair which they cannot effect
for themselves. In doing this I shall stay as close as possible to
my own experience, particularly as someone working with people
who have sought or been offered psychological help within
the facilities of the British National Health Service. I shall not
on the whole be considering the predicament of those thought
to have 'broken down' so seriously as to justify the label
'psychotic' and to merit admission for in-patient treatment (for
example for 'schizophrenia') in psychiatric hospitals – not
because I believe their condition is in any way fundamentally
different from that of the rest of us, but rather because my
experience in that kind of area is not particularly great. For the
most part, the people I have in mind may be experiencing quite
acute distress, in which 'anxiety' and 'depression' both feature
to some extent, perhaps taking a particular kind of form
('phobias', 'obsessions'), or seeming to them to indicate some
kind of – perhaps serious – physical illness. These are the kinds
of 'symptoms', in other words, which have been under scrutiny
throughout this book, and which will in some degree be familiar
to almost everyone.

The objectifying categories of thought which determine the
'symptoms' also, of course, determine the 'cures', so that the
mythology of 'breakdown' in the lay mind is complemented in
the professional mind by a mythology of 'treatment'. There is
something about operating within a common mythology which
seems in itself to have a kind of efficacy and to satisfy the
expectations of those involved whether or not there is any
independent evidence of anybody's really benefiting thereby –
indeed, the satisfaction of mythological expectations may in
itself constitute a certain kind of benefit. For example, one can
read accounts of medical treatments having been administered
throughout the ages to the obvious relief and satisfaction of
patients, even though, from our own scientific standpoint, the
treatments can at best have been neutral in terms of their

physical effects on patients. It would, I suggest, be simplistic to assume that physicians of previous ages were just wrong, while ours, with their superior 'scientific' insights, are right, and a sober consideration of history might well suggest that in any case ours may not be half as right as we like to think.* Science has become our own particular dogmatic mythology, and it is my belief that, while it may well perform the same kind of social functions which were served in previous times by magic, it now stands in the way of our achieving an accurate understanding of the origins and significance of psychological distress. There is a sense, then, in which the recognized professional approaches to 'breakdown' *work*, in that they provide a conceptual framework in which people's distress can be contained and dealt with. I do not wish to dismiss the significance of this kind of efficacy, but nor am I particularly interested in it, for whether or not the orthodox approaches 'work', they still, I believe, obscure the nature of our reality.

The kinds of help available to people whose distress drives them to seek it nearly all have their roots in a mechanistic (basically medical) view of 'illness' or 'breakdown'. In the long run, I think, this is bound to have negative effects since it serves the aims of a defensive objectification which can only mask from us realities of our world to which sooner or later we shall have to pay attention. But it also seems clear that there are good humanitarian reasons for the development and endurance of the mechanistic approach, and at least patients may expect to be able to reveal their distress without receiving an immediately moralistic or condemnatory response – although there is a small (and diminishing) risk that the person they are likely to consult first (their general practitioner) will respond with a 'pull yourself together' homily.

There are two main approaches to 'treatment' which are likely to be encountered once the plunge has been taken and the doctor consulted. The first is frankly medical, involving the prescription of physical treatments (particularly tranquillizing and anti-depressant drugs), and will be administered either by the general practitioner or by a psychiatrist to whom the patient has been referred. Prescription of treatment of this kind is likely to take place in a setting in which the patient will be expected to talk about 'symptoms' and personal difficulties, but probably not in any great detail or depth (as much, perhaps, as may be fitted into the odd ten- or fifteen-minute interview). The

* See I. Illich, *Medical Nemesis*, Calder & Boyars, 1975.

other main approach will focus more on the psychological 'causes' of the patient's difficulties, seeing them as the outcome of his or her life history and current situation, and is more likely to be taken by a psychiatrist or clinical psychologist to whom the patient has been referred. Although on the face of it less obviously 'medical' or mechanistic, these forms of treatment, as I shall argue in more detail presently, still depend heavily on inexplicit but distinctly medical assumptions.

The various schools and shades of opinion within these two broad approaches – in particular the variations to be found in the psychological therapies – are bewilderingly numerous, and the uninitiated sufferer, unless unusually well equipped with a knowledge of the field permitting insistence on a particular type of treatment (which even then may well not be available locally) is likely to receive nothing more reliable than pot luck once he or she enters the 'system'. The most predictable aspect of the treatment system, as well as the most prevalent, is that offered by orthodox psychiatry.

British psychiatry has on the whole stayed much closer to the traditions of physical medicine than has, for example, psychiatry in the USA, and those who rely for their expectations of psychiatrists on trans-Atlantic films or television programmes will be in for a surprise. Psychiatrists in Britain are trained in the orthodox methods of medicine, in which great emphasis is laid on the accurate identification (diagnosis) of illnesses, or 'disease entities', so that established methods of treatment can be applied almost automatically. Although many voices both within and outside psychiatry have been raised to suggest that this approach is not appropriate to much of the field of what has come to be called 'mental illness', the very rigidity of the deeply embedded practices and assumptions of medicine has meant that psychiatrists have been slow to react to doubts about the viability of their undertaking, and even when they have acknowledged that there may be conceptual difficulties about seeing 'problems of living' as illnesses, have not seemed able to think of anything more effective to *do* than administer superficial reassurance along with the tranquillizers.

There are, however, several factors which contribute to the maintenance of orthodox psychiatric practice other than simple lack of imagination on the part of psychiatrists. For example, it undoubtedly *is* possible to 'discover' systematic similarities and differences in the way people cope with distress, and it is therefore *plausible* to treat the revealed regularities as 'syndromes' resembling those more fruitfully identified in other fields of medicine. It is, however, frequently overlooked that the reliable identification of such 'behavioural' syndromes does not *necessarily* imply the presence of actual disease. Again, it would be quite wrong to pretend that 'psychotropic' drugs of the kinds prescribed by psychiatrists do not alter the way people experience the world through their bodily engagement with it, and that the contact they have with it may not by this means be rendered less painful. In some senses, at least, it is thus quite reasonable to acknowledge that physical treatments 'work', and it is also possible that the degree of relief experienced, apart from the obvious welcome it may be given by patients, may provide people with the opportunity to examine and deal with their predicament more effectively than they could when overwhelmed by anxiety or distress. It is also true, however, that many patients experience psychotropic medication as in itself a further source of confusion and discomfort, since it may alter their perception of the world in an idiosyncratic way, so that their experience seems to bear no relation to the meaning of the actual events of their world. Most patients whom I have seen, even when they have found the consumption of such medication helpful, seem to have a guilty sense of dependence on an almost illicit form of comfort of which they feel they should rid themselves.

I suspect that the argument that temporary reliance on tranquillizers or anti-depressants may permit patients to take a more effective grasp on their difficulties, while occasionally justified, in fact reflects an infrequent occurrence. The effect of such drugs seems on the whole to make one care less, not more, about the circumstances of one's life (which are in any case often extremely resistant to easy alteration) and hence to encourage an attitude which is even less likely than before to confront them. A little later in this chapter I shall be discussing factors common to *all* forms of psychiatric and psychological treatment which may result in the achievement of positive 'therapeutic gains' for patients, but for the present one might speculate that one of the central reasons for the continuing 'popularity' of orthodox psychiatry is the close correspondence of its assumptions to those of our cultural mythology.

There is little that is compellingly rational in the historical development of psychiatry's treatment techniques – the history of ECT (electro-convulsive therapy), for example, is a grotesque tale of mistaken assumptions and fortuitous observations (to do with the electrical stunning of Italian pigs before slaughter), from which emerges, in our day, the 'scientific' use of ECT on patients suffering from some forms of 'depressive illness'. Psychiatric treatments seem always to have been particularly prone to vicissitudes of fashion, underpinned by superficially plausible rationales that quite quickly turn out to be untenable. (Psychosurgery for schizophrenia, for example, once all the rage, is now virtually never used for this purpose, and indeed is, mercifully, not greatly in vogue for any psychiatric condition at present.) There is no convincing evidence that this is any less the case now than it ever was, and psychiatric theories about the causation of 'illnesses' such as 'schizophrenia', let alone the more heterogeneous 'neuroses', are signally lacking in scientifically persuasive force. In relation to their colleagues in other medical specialities, most psychiatrists are uncomfortable and defensive about the insubstantial basis of their discipline, and yet probably few of them (and few of their patients) doubt that they are on the right lines, since it seems 'obvious' that one day 'mental' and 'behavioural' 'disorders' will be shown to have physical causes which can be accurately diagnosed and effectively treated by physical means.

This reasoning is of course at the very centre of our self-characterization as machines, and the promise that our unhappiness can be relieved with little effort from ourselves by the administration of drugs, electricity, or brain surgery has a particularly strong appeal to our longing for passive objectivity. However, as has been pointed out by critics of the psychiatric orthodoxy such as Thomas Szasz, the cogency of this undertaking rests on the assumption that what are in fact 'disorders' of conduct, i.e. *moral actions*, can be traced to 'dysfunctional' mechanisms rather than accepted as the natural outcome of a person's transactions with the world. The man-as-machine analogy may be a fruitful one to apply in some areas of physical medicine, but there is certainly nothing *necessarily* compelling about its use in psychiatry.

The 'objective methodology' of research in psychiatry, as well as in other areas of the 'treatment' of 'mental disorder', precludes any radical criticism of the approaches involved since it assumes their conceptual validity at the outset – i.e., it only *looks for* entities of the type it *expects* to find. Briefly, methods of research perhaps most useful for determining, say, the relative usage of instant versus real coffee in different social *groups* or geographical areas (and therefore for suggesting likely marketing strategies), are used to supply inferences about the significance and reaction to treatment of an *individual's* personal psychological pain. Objective research deals almost exclusively with groups, statistical averages, artificially numerical measurement and predetermined categories of meaning (for example, diagnostic 'inventories' allow only a narrow range of answers to predetermined and usually highly specific questions). Within this framework there is no scope for voicing a *subjective* criticism of the procedures involved, and so what people actually think of themselves, their difficulties, or their treatment, is almost impossible to discover. (The reader may well be familiar with the related phenomenon which dictates that what is seen as being medically the matter with individuals depends far less on their subjective experience than on the 'objective' findings of X-rays, etc., so that people may even *themselves* discount their only too vividly experienced pain because it does not receive 'official' – objective – confirmation.) The 'scientific' studies of psychiatric procedures which fill the libraries to bursting point with ever-increasing numbers of 'learned journals' on the whole simply ignore how patients perceive their treatment, in favour of, for example, displaying a 'statistically significant difference' in some kind of 'objective measure' (such as a rating scale, questionnaire, psychological test score, etc.) between two or more groups of patients. The 'findings' of this huge volume of research literature are almost wholly equivocal.

My impression is that people on the whole are not greatly appreciative of the official methods of psychiatry, though this is not to say that many psychiatrists are not compassionate and experienced people who have at the very least the ability to offer support and reassurance to, and the power to arrange for a respite for, those in their care who have been particularly battered by their life experiences.

Those forms of 'treatment' which rest on a psychological rather than physical brand of mechanism constitute, as already mentioned, a very wide range of approaches which are not all that easily classified. Crudely, they may perhaps be split into two main strands: the 'psychodynamic' therapies which developed out of a tradition first established by Freudian psychoanalysis, and the 'behavioural' approaches which were developed more recently and have at least a significant part of their origins in the academic discipline of experimental psychology. There are also, however, many hybrid psychotherapies which draw their inspiration, often somewhat indiscriminately, from no particularly pure intellectual strain.

In the public mind 'psychotherapy' is often synonymous with psychoanalysis. However, despite the crucial role played by psychoanalysis in establishing a 'psychological' approach to the 'treatment' of 'mental disorder', orthodox Freudian analysis is not widely practised in Britain, and is only within the reach of a tiny minority of people who can afford the time and expense incurred in visiting an analyst several times a week over a period of years. There is a very small number of specialized clinics within the National Health Service which do owe particular allegiance to Freudian methods (though in a somewhat modified form), but it is extremely unlikely that the average patient will get anywhere near one.

It is much more likely that patients who are referred for specialized psychological therapy will find themselves receiving individual or group psychotherapy from psychiatrists (i.e. medically trained specialists) who have received instruction in psychotherapeutic 'techniques' loosely related to the Freudian approach, but considerably less intensive in terms of frequency and duration, or a form of 'behavioural' psychotherapy which is most likely to be dispensed by a clinical psychologist (i.e. a non-medical practitioner who has under- and post graduate training in psychology).

Although it is the later developed of the two broad strands of therapy to be considered here, it will be more convenient to consider the behavioural approach first; in any case, I think it probably true that this approach constitutes the most 'popular' and widely practised form of non-physical treatment likely to be encountered by the average patient.

Behaviourist psychology, from which behavioural psychotherapies derive many of their ideas and principles, was the ruling dogma in academic psychology in Britain and America for at least the middle forty years of this century (it seems fairly clear that in the academic, non-clinical field, this dogma is now giving way to slightly less simplistic, but still just as 'objective' variants on the man-as-machine theme). The central claim of behaviourism is that all those concepts which we connect with 'mind' (lumped together in the contemptuous term 'mentalism') are false, misleading, and (worst of all!) 'unscientific' because subjective and not measurable. We cannot therefore talk meaningfully of wishes, intuitions, desires, thoughts, feelings, intentions, etc., as long as these refer to people's subjective experience, since there is no way of demonstrating or measuring their existence objectively. If we are to be 'scientific', what we must do, therefore, is restrict ourselves to those aspects of people's *behaviour*, and the factors in the environment which impinge upon it, which are objectively observable and quantifiable. At the time when this view was being formulated, the concepts of the physiologist Pavlov were readily to hand to provide just the kind of objective characteristics which were needed to 'explain' 'behaviour' – i.e., stimulus, reponse, and the 'conditionable' connexion between them. The hope was that the behaviour of an individual person (referred to as 'the organism' in experimental jargon) could be predicted and controlled once a full understanding had been reached of the operation of the environmental stimuli which provoked from him or her what were seen (again according to Pavlov) as reflex responses.

For a number of reasons which are likely to be quite obvious to even the most unreflective layman, this attempt at producing an exact, experimental science of psychology was doomed to failure, not only because of the complexity needed to give a full account of human conduct in these terms (some very ingenious attempts were made to handle this) but also because, *in principle*, any such analysis is impossible unless the psychologist manages to become a different order of being from those whom he or she is studying (only God could be a successful behaviourist psychologist); the subject's *awareness* of the experimenter's predictions concerning the former's behaviour is, of course, often sufficient to change the very behaviour predicted. However, these philosophical stumbling blocks, which follow from the fact that psychologists are not gods and those they study are not machines, have not prevented the thriving development of behavioural methods in the clinical field.

Despite behaviourism's quite spectacular failure to produce a psychology which was either practically useful or intellectually convincing, psychologists' repetitious insistence on its 'scientificness' earned it a kind of superstitious credibility among those who had been brought up under its sway, and it was belief in this dogmatic claim which allowed some of its methods to be applied, and then vociferously advocated in the treatment of so-called 'neurotic' disorders. The field of non-physical treatment had up to that point (the late 1950s and early 1960s) been dominated by the medical, psychoanalytic approach, which, it is true, had maintained its dominance partly on the grounds of a mystique-laden appeal to what had become the rather convoluted theories which had been developed by his followers from Freud's often profoundly important insights. Behaviourally inclined clinical psychologists used the dogmatic appeal to scientific objectivism to challenge some of the more esoteric and impenetrable notions of the analysts and to offer instead a much simplified and altogether more obvious account of what caused, and what might cure, 'neurotic disorders'.

Rather than referring to, for example, the unconscious reaction to the Oedipal and castration complexes attaching to the repressed traumas of childhood, the unrecognized 'transference' longings of the infantilely fixated patient which it was the special business of the trained analyst to unravel, the behavioural therapist suggested that the neurosis consisted of nothing more than responses which had become faultily conditioned to inappropriate stimuli. The triumph of 'behaviour therapy', as it swiftly came to be called, was, under the guise of a 'scientific' technique of treatment, to appropriate the methods of common sense, and to turn the latter with good effect against some of the more mysterious, implausible and unhelpful practices of a psychoanalysis which had wandered too theoretically far from a basis in clinical experience.

In claiming to apply to clinical phenomena the 'laws of learning' which had been 'scientifically established' in university departments of psychology (claims almost laughable in their implausibility to all but the converted), behaviour therapists developed such 'techniques' as 'systematic desensitization' and 'implosion therapy'. Though set in a suitably impressive 'scientific' context which, for example, warned solemnly of the importance of the exact timing of 'reinforcement' (reward and punishment of 'responses'), etc., these proved to be nothing more than the time-honoured methods of overcoming anxiety either by a) being introduced very gradually to whatever causes it, or b) being thrown in at the deep end.

There is no doubt that there was a good deal that was helpful about this kind of approach, for example in demystifying some of the supposed powers of 'the shrink', and in (inadvertently) emphasizing the importance of bodily confrontation of those aspects of the real world which cause us distress. What was not helpful (and yet, ironically, lends behavioural methods much of their cultural acceptability) was the overtly, and even crassly, mechanistic nature of its theoretical claims.

Behaviour therapy, and related approaches such as

'behaviour modification', have enjoyed great popularity, spawning a wide variety of 'techniques' and a reputation for technical respectability which, though in my view entirely undeserved, is the envy of all its theoretical competitors. Of course, behaviour therapists' success, such as it actually is, may have very little to do with their theoretical position. While purportedly defining their patients' difficulties objectively, designing appropriate courses of intervention with scientific precision (for example by isolating those 'contingencies of reinforcement' – rewards and punishments – which maintain the 'dysfunctional behaviour' and replacing them with more appropriate ones) behaviour therapists are of course developing a relationship with patients which contains all kinds of elements which cannot *in fact* be conceptualized in the same aseptic and 'rigorous', 'non-mentalistic' terms as the theory itself. Behaviourist language, certainly, is as spotless as the scientist's proverbial white coat, studiously avoiding anything which smacks of imprecision or value judgment, but what behaviour therapists *do* is entirely another question – many of them are warm and concerned people whose conduct in the therapeutic setting bears only passing resemblance to their theoretical claims.

However effective behaviour therapists may be in their treatment of so-called 'neurotic disorders', they are to be numbered among the most prolific myth-makers of the age. The idea of the sufferer as a passive victim of a faulty 'learning history' (i.e. the inappropriate pairing of stimuli and responses), in principle repairable through a kind of re-programming not unlike that one might consider for a recalcitrant computer, clearly goes straight to the heart of our longing for machine status, as well as of the 'expert's' dream of technical mastery. It permits us also to continue to live uncritically in a world in which, it appears, people only go wrong more or less by accident. 'Evil' (if one may be permitted to use so emotive a word) thus becomes a technical, not a moral problem. Behavioural approaches share with most others which the sufferer is likely actually to come across an emphasis on the *individual's* malfunctioning in relation to a world which is taken as in essence objectively given and unalterable. That the world contains real evils which cause real distress which cannot simply be 'adjusted' out of individuals is countenanced as little by the behaviourists as by the other approaches under consideration, and indeed in its pure form behaviourism is perhaps the least likely of these approaches to allow any such possibility to be theoretically posed.

We must acknowledge, however, that the behavioural approach, having successfully masked common sense with a suitably 'scientific' façade, has in recent times modified its theoretical bases in order to try to avoid the embarrassment caused by some of its more obviously unacceptable simplistic assumptions. Behaviourally inclined psychologists have now had to acknowledge the importance of *meaning*, since they could not ignore for long the fact that, for instance, the same stimuli and responses may signify different things for different people, or to the same person at different times. The result of this is that there now exists a school – unthinkable to the pure behaviourist of old – known as 'cognitive behaviourism'. Where once 'mentalistic' concepts were anathema, 'cognitions' are now welcome, and behaviourists are happy to acknowledge that people think, and even to some extent initiate activity rather than simply react passively to 'environmental contingencies'. What has been preserved is a suitably impersonal, jargon-ridden, 'objective' language which gives proper regard to the dictates of mechanism. By taking compromising steps of this kind it seems to me that from a theoretical standpoint the approach has become less rather than more respectable, since now it is merely inconsistent, and the recognition of 'cognitions' seems to do little more than acknowledge, and then place far too much emphasis on, the fact that people 'talk' to themselves about what they are doing. Behaviourism would, I think, have done better to shift from 'behaviour' to 'conduct' (i.e. to acknowledge the moral possibility of *intention*) than to readmit under a new guise the mentalistic ideas which in some important ways it had been right to reject.

Therapeutically, the practice of cognitive behaviourism results in some fairly commonsense ideas about how patients may work at correcting faulty expectations or unduly pessimistic interpretations of their experience (for example by 'monitoring' and altering their 'self-talk'). This kind of approach seems to rest on assumptions to be found more generally in other forms of psychological therapy – e.g. that what matters (and what causes distress) is not so much the way things *are*, but the way things *seem*, and that by changing one's attitude towards them one may come to feel a good deal better. Since this is indeed a central aspect of most forms of psychological treatment, it may be as well to consider the more 'dynamic' approaches in somewhat greater detail before making any judgment about the usefulness of 'attitude change'.

As has already been pointed out, Freudian psychoanalysis, despite the familiarity of many of its concepts and even of its therapeutic method to the general public, is unlikely to be met with in anything like a pure form by those seeking help within the National Health Service. There are some psychiatrists (a minority) who practise group or individual therapy based loosely on psychoanalytic principles, and patients who fall into their hands may find their actions and utterances being 'interpreted' in the light of the unconscious motives which are supposedly to be detected beneath them, as well as a good deal of attention being paid to the 'transference' relationship between patient and therapist (i.e. the degree to which the patient carries over to that relationship feelings and expectations learned in earlier, particularly parental, relationships). The 'insight' to be gained from this therapeutic procedure will, it is hoped, lead either directly or indirectly to changes in the patient's actions.

Psychoanalytic theory is neither simple nor simplistic, and embedded in it is a view of human nature the implications of which have probably yet to be fully appreciated. A critique of psychoanalysis itself would take us too far beyond the purposes of the present book – suffice it to say for the moment that in my view only the foolish or the naive would treat psychoanalysis *as a theory* with anything but the greatest respect. As a practical technique in the hands of the less reflective therapist, however, it may leave a good deal to be desired. The temptation, of course, is to treat it as a technique which, mechanically applied, will lead automatically, and possibly mysteriously, to a 'cure' of the patient's 'neurosis'. Even more than with most forms of therapy, the analytic therapist may find it hard to resist the role of awe-inspiring expert, since so much of the theory is easily (if wrongly) seen as esoteric knowledge available only to a privileged few. For patients, this inscrutability of both theory and practitioner may be somewhat intimidating, or perhaps irritating, or possibly just baffling. However, there is, again, nothing to suggest that therapists claiming a theoretical allegiance to psychoanalysis may not be sensitive and concerned individuals whose experience over the years has given them a profound understanding of people in distress and has led to their developing helpful therapeutic practices which may or may not be related to Freudian theory.*

* For the views of a psychotherapist who has developed a very coherent account of his theoretical progress *beyond* his origins in psychoanalysis, see P. Lomas, *The Case for a Personal Psychotherapy*, Oxford University Press, 1981.

Post-Freudian psychotherapies, developed mainly by psychologists and psychiatrists in the USA, have probably had more
influence on the kind of non-medical, non-behavioural, psychological help available through official channels in Britain.
Among these are Carl Rogers's 'client-centred therapy', George
Kelly's 'personal construct therapy', Albert Ellis's 'rational-
emotive therapy', Eric Berne's 'transactional analysis' and
Fritz Perls's 'Gestalt psychotherapy' (the two latter approaches
probably enjoy greater popularity beyond rather than within
the 'official' setting of the National Health Service). It is not
easy to generalize about these approaches, not least because
it is usually one of the central aims of any 'school' of psychotherapy precisely to *differentiate* itself from other schools.
However, most of them do, I think, share a particular focus on
the *individual* and the way he or she experiences the world.

This exploration of how the person sees his or her predicament takes place in a setting in which the importance of the
*quality* of the relationship between therapist and patient is
explicitly recognized, and there is no doubt that this is an
advance (attributable in particular to Rogers) over those 'techniques' which (like orthodox psychoanalysis) advocated in
accordance with the best mechanistic principles a deliberately
impersonal role for the therapist. Thus the therapist's personal
way of relating to the patient – for example, to use Rogers's
terms, with warmth, empathy and genuineness – becomes central to the therapeutic process rather than an aspect of it
deliberately to be expunged.

It is a central point of all psychotherapies that patients' views
concerning what ails them will be questioned by the therapist,
perhaps even disputed quite hotly (many therapies lay emphasis on the importance of *confronting* patients with the falsity
of their views). This I see as a necessary part of *undeceiving*
people about the mythological accounts of their difficulties
which they have come to tell themselves, but it is easy to slip
from this position to one which takes an almost entirely relati-
vistic view about the way people see the world. Undeceiving
someone is, usually, to present them with a view of the world
which is clearer, more accurate, than the mythified (defensive)
view with which they deceived themselves, but also a *painful*
one which requires some kind of active (bodily) response from
them; it is *not* simply to replace a 'maladjusted' or somehow
distressingly misconceived view of their circumstances with a
more reasonable (rational) one which shows them that things

are not so bad really, or that all their difficulties have been due to their mistaken way of looking at things. This latter, and, I think, misguidedly optimistic view of psychological distress is a characteristic of many of the lighter-weight psychotherapies at the 'cognitive' end of the spectrum. At the root of such approaches, again, is an almost entirely mechanistic view of man, in which adjustments to *individuals* (changing attitudes or perceptions, training in 'skills') are, even if no more than tacitly, seen as the way to tackle what are in fact absolutely *real* difficulties arising *between* people and the world. If taken at their face value, such approaches are cruelly mythifying, since the person is left in a painful world with nothing more substantial than the belief that if only he or she could see it differently things would be better.

It is no surprise that any seriously conducted psychological investigation of people in distress will quickly run across the importance of the way such people interpret their world (i.e., what they tell themselves about it), and in this is to be found the defensiveness (self-deception) which Freud's inquiries so clearly revealed. That such investigation has almost always taken place in the context of fundamental assumptions having their origin in medico-mechanistic habits of thought (including, for instance, ideas of 'breakdown' and 'cure') means, however, that the significance of what is being defended *against* is over-looked. The individual defends against a painful world, and it all too easily happens that the therapist concentrates on the 'maladaptive' nature of the defences, aiming to 'cure' the person of reliance on them, but ignoring the moral problem presented by the world's real dangers and injustices against which they have been erected. Whether they know it or not, and however much they might wish to repudiate such a role, psychological therapists almost inevitably become instruments for the adjustment of individuals to a social *status quo*.

It is perhaps implicit in the work of those who, like R. D. Laing and Thomas Szasz, have criticized the 'mental health' approach to psychological distress that any therapist who accepts that something is *wrong with* those who seek help is likely to be implicated in a moral-political confidence trick. Only the therapist who adopts the position that there is *nothing* wrong with those in distress (i.e. no mechanical or even 'cognitive' fault identifiable), but that their response is a *natural* one to a painful world, stands a chance of not enmeshing people even further in the strands of myth.

Enormous efforts have been made to determine what if anything is useful and helpful in the various kinds of treatment
available to those who seek it. Almost all this research has, as
one might expect, been carried out within the 'scientific' tradition which asserts the values of objectivity and mechanism.
The search has thus been for techniques, stimuli, controllable
and generalizable therapeutic strategies which will lead to
predictable improvement in the identifiable 'conditions' 'presented' by patients. Everything about the therapeutic effort,
from the construction of technique-specifying theories to the
painstaking effort to demonstrate their effectiveness through
objective research, testifies to the fundamentally mechanist
assumptions involved. There are undoubtedly very many people
so embedded in this perspective that they would consider it
barely sane to question it – it seems to them simply *self-evident*
that the kinds of 'symptoms' which those in distress display just
must be due to specific causes which can at least in principle be
understood and eradicated by technical experts. Even the most
'humanistic' psychological theories tend to betray an allegiance
to this kind of belief, even if they do not profess it.

In the final analysis it is only a profound mechanistic faith
of this kind which can explain the extent to which the professionalization of psychological help has taken and is taking
place. Professional helping organizations sprout and mushroom
in direct proportion to the rate at which people embrace a conception of themselves as mechanical objects. Experiencing themselves as unloved and without resources, drained of energy,
powerless, blistered by the omnipresent gaze of the threatening
Other, unable to meet the standards objectively established for
beauty and effectiveness, struggling with conditions of life
which, if accepted as objectively immovable, appear to a view
unclouded by myth as almost unbearably malign, people naturally turn hopefully to the only kind of remedy their cosmology
permits them to imagine: i.e., one which offers mechanical
modification to adjust them to the world.

The fundamental social conceptions of our time of course play
straight into the interests of the 'helping professions', and the
search for security in objectivity offers those of us involved in
mediating its delivery an opportunity for profit which only the
most self-denying could refuse. As long as therapists can see
themselves as 'change agents', possessors of 'therapeutic skills',
'trained' and 'qualified' in technical procedures firmly grounded
in a scientific 'knowledge base', able to offer 'programmes' of

'treatment' and courses of 'training in social skills', to correct 'sexual dysfunction' through behavioural 'techniques' of established effectiveness, and so on and on, they can scarcely be chided for taking money for their services.

In fact, however, there is not a shred of convincing evidence in support of these or similar claims, and there can be no doubt that they continue to be asserted not least because the interests of a professional helping industry have become a barrier to appreciating the truth. Again I would wish to stress, however, that this is not the sole reason for the way things are, or even the most important (even those who advocate 'self-help therapy' as an alternative to over-professionalized approaches still for the most part see 'therapy' as a *technical* undertaking). The helpers have as big a 'religious' stake as the helped in the mythology of objectivity, and most would feel a quite sincere pride in the humanitarian nature of their calling. To question the motives of therapists' conduct is no less challenging and painful – possibly outraging – to them than it is for them to do the same with their patients in the course of therapy, but neither is it intended to carry any greater imputation of blame. If patients can only get to grips with the world by becoming aware of the context from which their experience stems, so therapists cannot in the long run afford morally to ignore the significance of their conduct *as* therapists while priding themselves (not unjustifiably) on their conduct in easing people's pain *in* therapy.

Despite what I take to be the fact that there is no consistent evidence for the effectiveness of psychiatric and psychological intervention as technical treatment, there can be little doubt that many of those offering such treatment are in fact experienced by their patients as helpful. The reasons for this are clear enough for all to see, but have largely been ignored because they do not accord with our mythology. Even many of the most 'objective' research studies of therapeutic methods have acknowledged, often with a kind of apologetic puzzlement, that the personal qualities of therapist and patient, and the nature and quality of the relationship between them, are influential in determining the degree to which 'treatment' is found to be useful. Because such factors form no part of the technical procedures held by most (but not all) therapeutic theorists to be important, they are often more or less dismissed as 'non-specific' by research workers and commentators. It also seems likely that the realities of the situation in which therapy takes place encourage therapists to conduct themselves in ways more consistent than the theoretical differences between them would seem to permit: in other words, people of reasonably good will whose professional lives expose them to the kinds of experiences of people and their difficulties which are in fact familiar to therapists are likely to end up doing much the same kinds of things with patients no matter what they tell themselves they are doing. There is as evidence of this, research work which suggests that experienced therapists of different theoretical allegiances in fact conduct themselves more similarly in therapy than do experienced and inexperienced therapists of the same school. For these and similar reasons it may be sensible to seek a 'de-mythified' account of what people in distress do actually find helpful, rather than straining our credulity on accounts which seem to be aimed more at supporting the structures of objectivity than articulating our experience.

In fact there is quite a large, but also largely neglected, literature which attempts to take therapists' and patients' experiences seriously.* The basic lessons of therapeutic experience, seriously reflected upon, can, I believe, be stated in outline quite succinctly, though they have implications for a long overdue renewal of interest in subjectivity which need to be spelt out in considerable detail, and will in fact form the focus of the final two chapters of this book. There is, however, one particular problem presented by the professional practice of an 'honest' psychotherapy (i.e. one which, among other things, starts out on the basis that there is nothing *wrong with* the individuals who are helped by it) from which even the most serious and socially committed of its practitioners have tended to deflect their attention. Before addressing this particular difficulty, however, it would be as well briefly to sketch what appear to be the main features of psychological therapies which seem actually to be of help (though much of this will I hope by now be apparent from previous discussion in this book).

Psychological help, then, is gained by those who seek it first and foremost in the context of a *relationship* in which they are *undeceived* about the nature and significance of a real, often complex and possibly insolubly difficult, painful predicament or set of circumstances, and *encouraged* to confront *bodily* those aspects of the predicament which admit of any possibility of change. In essence this procedure is a moral, not a technical

* For two recent attempts of this kind see P. Lomas's book, already referred to, and my own *Psychotherapy: A Personal Approach*, Dent, 1978.

undertaking, since at every point it necessitates judgments' being made by both therapist and patient about what is *right* and what is *good* for either or both to do, not only in the immediate therapeutic setting, but also in the wider social context (particularly, of course, that of the patient). I do not believe that this process can be stated, evaluated or understood in the conventionally objective terms which determine our orthodox habits of thought, and therefore all sorts of questions must be raised and revisions made concerning what we usually take to be the nature of responsibility, learning, 'breakdown', etc. Some of these questions have already been addressed, others will be shortly. What needs to be considered now (and raises the particular difficulty mentioned above) is the implications of the nature of the *relationship* upon which effective 'therapy' seems to depend, and how this can be reconciled with a *professional* stance on the part of therapists.

In the semi-technicized jargon of some of the more 'humanistic' therapies, it has, as already indicated, been recognized that personal qualities of therapists like 'unconditional positive regard' (warmth), 'accurate empathy', and 'congruence' (genuineness), seem conducive to positive change in 'clients'. That these are seen as 'qualities' *possessed* by therapists (thereby stimulating attempts to 'train' people in their acquisition) testifies to the tacit influence of the philosophy of objectification, for they are of course qualities of *relationship* which may be abstracted from people's *conduct* towards each other, but which cannot be turned into things or possessions. However, the central conclusion to be drawn from such observations is that people are most likely to be influenced positively by those whom they trust, and have *reason* to trust. This has, indeed, been acknowledged quite unflinchingly by several psychotherapists of great distinction (C. G. Jung being among the earliest), and the bravest have gone as far as venturing the view that the most important 'healing' force in the therapeutic equation is *love*.*

The very breath of such a notion is of course enough to send the orthodox technicians of psychotherapy scurrying behind the ramparts of objectivity, from where it can safely be regarded as preposterous nonsense. If true, however, we come

* See, for example, I. D. Suttie, *The Origins of Love and Hate*, Penguin Books, 1960, and P. Lomas, *True and False Experience*, Allen Lane, 1973. Paul Halmos, in an important but now largely overlooked work, *The Faith of the Counsellors*, Constable, 1965, examined in considerable detail the importance of love in therapy.

face to face with the difficulty (alluded to above) which I think even the bravest therapists prefer not to confront: is it morally justifiable that patients should (directly or indirectly) *pay* for the professional provision of love?

Once all the technical mystique has been stripped away from psychotherapy, it does seem that a likely explanation for its almost explosive expansion over the last few decades is that it provides something which is otherwise in very short supply in a world in which a kind of watchful defensiveness against our vulnerability has replaced any kind of spontaneous generosity which people may more often once have felt for each other. As Peter Lomas, particularly in *True and False Experience*, has very cogently argued, the good therapist's stance towards his or her patients may be likened to that of good parents towards their children. This may perhaps be described as a kind of unselfish, loving concern and interest under the benign influence of which the child (or patient) can grow into an adult person. It is precisely this kind of intense, concerned, caring interest which is in such short supply in our objectifying social world – even, if not especially, in the place where one would most hope to find it, i.e., between parents and children. The demands of our social organization, the threat of annihilation which necessitates the toughening of our defences, the unrelenting competitiveness which the need for objective status provokes, all militate against our addressing each other spontaneously with the kind of open, subjective, personal, intuitive, honest lovingness which we find so warming but so scarce.

So depleted are our resources, so needy are we of the sort of loving attention which is like rain to a meadow, that we cannot find the strength to offer this kind of attention to others in our personal lives, but feel an almost overwhelmingly insistent demand to receive it from them which is of course never met, since they are like us. The only times we are likely to experience the warmth we crave is for those relatively fleeting periods when our interests appear to coincide with those of another (as may be the case with mother and infant, or between lovers). Almost everyone is desperate to be recognized, confirmed, approved. Just as it can annihilate with a cold stare, so can the Other through a loving glance infuse the flagging spirit with life-giving warmth. But our neediness prevents us from being Other for others.

The psychotherapist, in fact, offers a commodity available almost nowhere else (not, that is, with any consistency or predictability). Quite regularly, for about an hour at a time, you can go to your psychotherapist and be listened to, concentrated upon, thought about, puzzled over, understood, questioned, encouraged. Here is someone who will take an absolutely exclusive interest in you (or so, certainly, it is likely to seem to you), who will attend to and remember even apparently trivial details of your life, who will sympathize with your pain even when gently remonstrating with instances of your intransigence, who will blame you for nothing and demand nothing from you, fob you off with no superficial or impossible advice, but open the way for you to tackle the difficulties in your life. Put like this, surely, it is not hard to see the attraction of psychotherapy nor to understand its popularity, and scarcely necessary to invent for it any spuriously technical justification. The more therapists' interest and concern is genuine (as opposed to the rather coldly distant professional posture which some earlier psychotherapists took to be proper), the more they appear as real, recognizable people, the more they are likely to be trusted, and the more effective their influence – just as loving, and lovable, parents will have more influence over children than punitive, forbidding, or indifferent ones. Just such inferences as these are to be drawn from research revealing the 'non-specific' factors in psychotherapy.

There are of course qualities brought by good therapists to psychotherapy other than *merely* concern and warmth, just as the good parent will need more for the successful upbringing of children than simply benignly approving affection. Love, perhaps, is more than just a *component* in a 'therapeutic package', but rather the *spirit in which* one person places his or her resources at the disposal of another. Just as parents place at the disposal of their children, among other things, their knowledge of the world, in a way which maximizes the usefulness of that knowledge, bending their concern to the child's interests, so therapists use their knowledge of, say, the nature and significance of distress, in their patients' interests. As professional people therapists are not more effective than laymen because of any greater capacity to love (and certainly not because of any esoteric technical knowledge), but rather because of the opportunity open to them to draw on their special experience in a loving way. That they can *afford* to be loving in this way may at least in part be attributed to the undemanding and uncomplicated nature of the emotional setting in which professional therapy takes place. If their relationship with patients extended beyond the times at which they made themselves professionally available, therapists would then end up in the same boat as all those who find *mutually* demanding relationships so threatening and draining.

Therapists are naturally quick to point out the importance for successful therapy of the professional nature of their engagement with patients, but are on the whole less comfortable about acknowledging the moral incongruity of offering, in essence, love for money. Psychotherapists in private practice often profess a convenient belief that patients are only properly 'motivated' to make the kind of efforts necessary for therapeutic progress if they pay for their therapy, but few of those who fully appreciate the importance of love to their calling are quite as brazenly and unreflectively self-interested, though they would still, I think, be reluctant to admit that their activities served any but the highest of motives. However, my own feeling is that it may be salutary for those of us who make a living as psychotherapists to consider the wider implications of what we do, for there is no obvious reason to suppose that ours is less disabling as a profession than any other.

Almost anything in our society which can be turned into a commodity and marketed, will be. Love is no exception to this rule, and it can come as no surprise that in a world in which its free availability is so strictly limited there should be found a flourishing profession engaged in its supply. This is again, of course, not the result of a conscious plot on the part of unusually greedy or unscrupulous individuals, but rather the inevitable outcome of the interplay of supply and demand, needs and interests.

In this way, then, I think it not entirely shocking to suggest that psychotherapists are to be found in a role closely analogous to that of prostitutes. As a professional group prostitutes may not commonly be held in great social esteem, but probably few would claim that, in a less than perfect world, their activities are entirely without social value. (If nothing else, prostitution has the merit of honesty; for this reason it is sad to learn that there are apparently prostitutes in the USA who have now begun to call themselves 'sex therapists'!)

Just as prostitutes supply sexual favours to those who find them difficult to obtain in any other way, so psychotherapists provide for a price the kind of individual attention many of us need to get from someone in order to survive in a cruel world. Therapists may feel that the attention (love) they give their patients is more genuine, more worthwhile and respectable than the sexual 'love' dispensed by prostitutes. But this, I think, is debatable. The prostitute's is a very specific and very frank service – though she may not feel love for her clients, she unequivocally makes her body available to them on terms which are clearly understood. She may well feign an affection or enthusiasm she doesn't feel, but such deception, even if necessary for the successful conduct of her business, is perhaps relatively innocent and uncomplicated. The psychotherapist, on the other hand, may be helping patients through the provision of what they experience (even if inarticulately) as love, but under the guise of performing a psychological service of a *technical* nature. In this way psychotherapists may be appropriating their patients' ability to understand their own situation and think clearly about themselves, and by technicizing, and in fact mythifying, psychological understanding they make it the property of a professional class – that is, they become 'professional usurers' in the way discussed in the previous chapter. Furthermore, the love through which their therapeutic function is *actually* achieved is but a pale and uncommitted version of what it would be in an ideal world, but is not *acknowledged* as such. Patients, it is true, may sometimes ruefully comment that 'you wouldn't put up with me if you weren't being paid to', and most therapists would be unlikely to deny, at least to themselves, that this is indeed the case; however, when not faced directly with this element of hypocrisy, therapists are quite likely sentimentally to deceive themselves about the 'deeply meaningful' significance of the therapeutic relationship.

It is certainly true that the therapist can become a figure of enormous importance to patients, often because he or she seems to them to be the only person who cares, and most competent therapists are aware of the dangers and responsibilities of this role. Almost none of them, of course, assume that in *reality* they could be this important or would be willing to shoulder the responsibility of so being – rather, they have convenient psychological 'mechanisms', such as 'the transference', readily at hand to 'explain' their patients' degree of dependence, infatuation, etc. No doubt it is possible for therapists at least unconsciously to abuse their role – to become a kind of paid friend and confidant to patients, endlessly taking their money in exchange for an available ear, a tolerant acceptance of their transgessions, an interested but morally uncritical acceptance of their interpersonal and sexual preoccupations and worries, offering appropriately mysterious psychological 'interpretations' which provide a kind of scientific justification for an anxious or tedious, or even profligate or futile life. Much more likely, however, is the kind of situation where the therapist simply slides into the role of substitute parent or friend, thereby indirectly siphoning off from the world − absolutely without meaning to do so − people's ability to support and look after each other. To turn love into a commodity, especially without realizing that that is what is being done, may turn out to be one of the most disabling professional feats of all. On the other hand, to recognize that the provision of therapeutic love in a far from perfect world may be better than nothing at all, to accept, that is, that psychotherapy is like a form of prostitution, may be to achieve a quite healthy perspective.

If one accepts our present social organization and ways of thinking about ourselves as more or less immutable, and if one can see no alternative to the structure and mode of influence of our social and intellectual institutions, then it seems likely to me that the only palliative to what appears to be an increasingly psychologically distressing and painful existence for most people is going to be an ever-expanding profession of love-givers of one kind or another. Apart from this, presumably, our only recourse may be to strengthening our defences by reinforcing our mythology (to a point at which we shall be in danger of becoming subjectively detached from the external world), or simply blowing ourselves up and starting, if possible, again. However, after only a few hundred years of anything like carefully recorded and reflective intellectual and moral development, it may seem premature to presuppose that radical changes in our understanding of ourselves and our relations with each other and with the world are not possible. Contemptuous though one might be about utopianism (and it is certainly the case that we cannot foresee with any accuracy at all what conceptual turns our descendants may take), we certainly have no reason to be self-satisfied about the present, as anyone who has the courage to examine the reality behind the myth must, in my view, acknowledge. It may not therefore be entirely idle to consider ways in which the experience of some of those involved in often very painful self- (and other-) examination point to revisions we may profitably make in our approach to the world and what we tell ourselves about it, even if some of these cut across our most cherished and 'objectively well established' beliefs. Perhaps one of the most pressing problems confronting us is to conceive of ways in which people may regain personal dignity and effectiveness in a social world in which there is not, and never will be, enough love to go round.

# 8   The Possibility of Undeception

Before it is possible to formulate even a vague idea of how one may be able to live one's life constructively (though certainly not painlessly) and *relatively* free of the paralysis which anxiety and psychological distress often impose (though certainly not free of fear, uncertainty and worry), it is necessary first to be able to expose the falsity of our usual way of looking at ourselves in relation to our world.

The equipment needed for undeceiving ourselves is not readily to hand, since culturally we have for centuries put all our conceptual eggs in the basket of objectivity, and it is the concepts of objectivity which we have used as the main means of our self-deception. To find our way back to judging ourselves and the world from a defensibly subjective standpoint means entertaining ideas and exercising faculties which we have all but forgotten how to name. But there *are* ways of knowing which are independent of objective language, and there *are* meanings other than objective meanings; one *can* make valid judgments on the basis of evidence unendorsed by 'experts', indeed one can appreciate truths which are unavailable to objectivity. Most important of all we can *share* subjective forms of knowledge, meaning and truth: it is one of the crasser, and most harmful, notions of objectivity to identify subjectivity with solipsism, to suggest, that is, that subjective experience is necessarily idiosyncratic, untrustworthy and incommunicable (on our first day as first-year psychology students, a lecturer told us, with almost savage satisfaction, that from that day forth, if we wanted to be scientists, we must forget our own personal experience as far as the pursuit of psychological understanding was concerned). It is of course true that subjective, personal opinions, beliefs and explanations can have no particular claim to truth, and are certainly of little interest to science; subjective *experience*, on the other hand, is in the long run the only ground upon which truth can rest.

Perhaps our greatest frustration is caused by our inevitable failure to achieve the goals which our myths tell us must be achieved. We believe in love (of the 'object-confirming' kind), we believe in 'relationships', we believe in 'fulfilment' (material, sexual, and sometimes even spiritual), we believe in happiness, and we see all of them as objective, obtainable possessions without at least some of which our lives will be rendered barren and meaningless. When the failure to achieve such goals leads our subjectivity to nudge our awareness with dread, when we find ourselves frozen under the gaze of the Other or threatened with annihilation by the withdrawal of love, there seems to be no refuge, nowhere to struggle to where existence can be continued. In the final chapter of this book I shall make some tentative suggestions about alternative ways of dealing with our predicament, but first of all, in this chapter, I shall try to draw together themes, many of which have been introduced earlier, to make a little clearer how we may at least begin to think about ourselves in ways which are not determined by our deep-seated penchant for objectivity and machine status.

I have already tried to establish that there is nothing particularly trustworthy about the words with which we consider our experience, and indeed that what we tell ourselves about our experience is more rather than less likely to serve the aims of self-deception. 'Anti-subjectivity' may make use of the fact that the possibilities for self-deception are infinite to suggest that the experience which underlies them is itself untrustworthy. But this, I think, is wrong, and in fact robs us of the only chance we have to *share* experience. The only acceptable form of objectivity is that which arises out of the overlapping of our individual subjectivities. Even for physical science, the ultimate test of whether or not something is true lies in the individual's experience, not in some objectified, dogmatic set of rules. The sensory experiences which are predictable from natural scientific 'laws' permit agreement between individuals because those individuals share very similar physical structures, are persuaded by the same kinds of logical reasoning, and operate with a similar set of values. It is easy to forget that, for example, it is only because scientists *value* the evidence of their senses that science itself hangs together; for a religious person who values, say, only the authority of holy writ, scientific statements need not be in the least compelling. The nature of our embodied presence in the world, i.e., the structure of our bodies in relation to the structure of the world, must in large part determine what one considers it important to know as well as the means of our getting to know it. We are able to build a shared body of scientific knowledge only in so far as we share this kind of common structure. Were they given the opportunities for self-conscious reflection conferred by language, other types of being (bees, say, or fish) would presumably construct a very different kind of science, because the nature of their engagement with the world is very different; the evidence of *their* senses would in many important respects differ greatly from the evidence of ours.

Science is thus not the creation of some kind of mysterious contact with or insight into ultimate reality, but the upshot of our own very human, and even culturally local, interests, concerns and values. I suspect, also, that we are ready to give particular weight and credence to the 'evidence of our senses' only because it is not in our interests to deceive ourselves about its nature (though it is certainly *possible* to do so). It is unfortunately much *more* in our interests to deceive ourselves about our subjective experience of our relations with and conduct towards each other, and indeed our intuitions of our own motives. We have, for example, as I have tried to suggest earlier, developed ways of considering, talking about and investigating our own motives which allow us the maximum scope for deception and self-deception, and we have almost entirely obscured from ourselves the insight that our motives are quite easily discoverable from our *conduct* (as opposed to our language).

In fact, I believe that our psychological, moral, social ways of experiencing are fundamentally *just as* shareable as our more obvious sensory experience. In other words, what I have called our 'intuitive sensitivity' is, I believe, just as reliable as the experience which provides the ultimate justification for natural scientific statements, but that, because of the problematic and painful nature of the world it reveals to us, we have chosen almost completely to suppress and ignore it in favour of a false objectivity. No doubt many would consider this an extreme claim, if not just a foolish one, but there does seem to me to be some evidence for it. For one thing, if it were not the case that we shared an extremely elaborate, fine, delicate awareness of the interpersonal, moral, unsayable currents that flow between us, and between us and the world, we should not in fact be able to sustain any kind of orderly conduct towards each other. How, for example, could one possibly negotiate the role of lover, or parent, or even buy a box of matches in the corner shop, according to the rules and precepts of objectivity alone? Even the most elaborate computers would not be able to cope with the subtlety of the *reality* which infuses even the simplest of human exchanges. For another thing, I have found that it *is* possible, even in the face of the most determined efforts at self-deception, to appeal to what people know, to ask people to *trust* their experience.

In the conduct of psychotherapy, for example, it is possible over and over again to see a patient struggling to deny what both he or she and the therapist know to be the case – the *reality* of the denied, the rock-solid certainty of what the patient is seeking to obscure, cannot for ever go unacknowledged precisely because it is so obvious, lying across their subjectivities at least as surely as the walls and windows which occur in both their visual fields, even though not 'objectively' demonstrable according to the tenets of 'scientific' dogma. I *know* if you are afraid of me, and I know you know I know, even should we deny it with our language and seek to cancel it out with our gestures. Centuries of effort to gainsay knowledge such as this means that we have lost the concepts – or failed to develop them – with which to consider it, but that does not alter the certainty of our knowledge. This is not, of course, to say that such knowledge is infallible or cannot be mistaken, just as the evidence of our senses can at times be misleading, but it *is* just as good as any other kind of knowledge.

We could, I think (and do in certain protected settings such as that found in psychotherapy), check, evaluate and elaborate the knowledge given by our intuitive sensitivity, but for that we need to be able to stand to each other in a relation of good faith, and our difficulty in achieving that constitutes the major stumbling block for the development and appreciation of inter-subjective truth. For a variety of reasons (which owe as much to chance as to any impersonally objective reality) you will be hard put to it to deny that there is a telephone on my desk, but if you wish to deny that you are afraid of me (when you are) you have every chance of obscuring the truth. In principle, the exercise of bad faith is equally *possible* in either situation, but much more in our interests to permit in the sphere of intuitive sensitivity. To be able to acknowledge the truth which is to be gained in this sphere, one has to *want* to find it.

To the objectivist mind there is no doubt something absolutely maddening about suggesting that one should *trust* one's 'intuitive sensitivity', since such a statement seems to lack all the verbal and 'operational' exactness which objectivity demands. The objectivist can tolerate such a concept only if the phenomena involved can be converted or translated into concrete and manipulable commodities (hence the attempted translation of some of the more subtle features of social interchange into a 'body language' which can be used consciously to manipulate or dissemble). However, the very nature of intui-

tive knowledge is such that it need not, and *cannot*, be translated in this way without the immediate loss of its essentially
subjective character: as soon as you become unspontaneous in
some particular sphere of conduct, your spontaneity slips away
to some other sphere, where again it operates, as it were, out of
self-conscious sight.

There is really nothing surprising about suggesting that
there can be fields of communicable meaning which cannot be
made articulate in language. Even if language bears almost the
entire weight of our (objective) intellectual culture, it is by no
means the only meaning-system with which we are familiar –
for example, musical experience is known, understood, com-
municated, evaluated and validated, in its own terms, quite
satisfactorily and fully without ever having to be put into
words. We feel no particular embarrassment about acknowledging and sharing musical meaning outside the context of
language, and its essentially non-linguistic nature does not
lead us to dismiss music as somehow unreliable and misleading.
We can of course *talk about* music, consider it verbally in every
aspect, but in doing so we do not feel we have to reject the
wordless experience of music itself.* I see no reason why we
should not extend the same validity to the experience rendered
us by our intuitive sensitivity.

Our objective habits of thought also demand that some
account be given of what could possibly be meant by 'intuitive
sensitivity' – for example, on what objective or mechanical
structures could it depend? Though I certainly mean to invoke
no mysterious or magical faculty, and while I am happy to
acknowledge that the exercise of such sensitivity must depend
upon the structures of our body and the evidence of our senses,
it does seem to me that perhaps it *cannot* be analysed in the
way which objectivity demands, since it lies at the very basis of
our knowledge of the world. Perhaps it is true that one can
know everything (or, at least, a great deal!) except how we
know – for as soon as we knew how we know, the process of our
knowing would again slip out of sight. Put at its simplest,
subject (knower) cannot simultaneously and for itself be object
(known). This kind of thought, familiar enough – indeed positively banal – in Continental philosophy, is by and large
anathema to the Anglo-Saxon mind, and yet it is hard to see

---

* The implications of this argument are spelt out in extremely interesting
detail by Susanne Langer, *Philosophy in a New Key*, Harvard University Press,
1942.

how it can be escaped, even if it seems to outrage what we have been taught to consider reason.

This philosophical problem is more than just an intellectual puzzle, and it is very easy to see how it translates into concrete reality. For as soon as objectivity unearths what it takes to be the fundamentals of our ways of knowing, it seeks to put them to practical use without noticing that *what* is putting them to use is again, inevitably, an unanalysed subject.

Not only, then, is it possible for us to trust in our subjective experience, but in the final analysis we have no alternative to doing so, though we can of course fail to acknowledge that we do so. Trust in one's experience, however, carries with it no objective guarantee of correctness, and as much as anything else it is probably the risk of being wrong which generated our desire for absolute objectivity. The objectivity which we created ended up, ironically, by dogmatically removing us – the knowers – from the scene altogether.

Where objective knowing is passive, subjective knowing is active – rather than giving allegiance to a set of methodological rules which are designed to deliver up truth through some kind of automatic process, the subjective knower takes a personal risk in entering into the meaning of the phenomena to be known. In learning to read, for example, the child takes a risk with those words he or she is unacquainted with, relying on the context for clues which *might* be misleading (it strikes me that children of the television age are often particularly reluctant to take this kind of risk – their reception of meaning needs somehow to be 'authorized' before they will risk 'knowing' it). One of the most 'subjectively risking' people I know tells with puzzlement how she is the only person in her particular circle who seems able to understand the West Indian patois of one of her neighbours. Needing to judge correctly means risking foolish mistakes, and trusting one's intuitive sensitivity demands a quality – courage – not normally associated with purely 'cognitive' activity. Objectivity, again, attempts to remove from our ways of knowing the necessity for courage.

When the risk is successfully taken, one reaches an inter-subjectively shared reality which is as concrete as any other, even though it may not be 'demonstrable' in objective terms. Seven members of a therapeutic group may know with absolute certainty that the eighth is falsely disavowing anger, but there is no really satisfactory way of 'proving' the case objectively; nevertheless, the *strength* of their case leads the eighth member to acknowledge its truth. He *could* of course be giving way to 'social pressure' (in which case the more sensitive members would probably know he was) but there can be no way of deciding this which depends on anything more solid than subjective certainty.

Those who have some time for the validity of subjective experience but intellectual qualms about any kind of 'truth' which is not 'objective', are apt to solve their problem by appealing to some kind of relativity. For example, it might be felt that we all have our own *versions* of the truth about which we must tolerantly agree to differ (I have already discussed some of the implications of this kind of view for psychotherapy in Chapter 7). While in some ways this kind of approach represents an advance on the brute domination of the 'objective truth', it in fact undercuts and betrays the *reality* of the world given to our subjectivity. Subjective truth has to be actively struggled for (just as, in psychotherapy, the truth of the patient's predicament has to be painfully negotiated): we need the courage to differ until we can agree.

Though the truth is not just a matter of personal perspective, neither is it fixed and certain, objectively 'out there' and independent of human knowing. 'The truth' changes according to, among other things, developments and alterations in our values and understandings. It is an act of unbelievable hubris to suppose that we have, or could have, a kind of contact with absolute objective Reality which guarantees us a truth which is independent of our interests. The idea of something approaching absolute or objective truth is one of the main weapons with which to defend dogma and to subdue those who wish to evolve our understanding. But the 'non-finality' of truth is not to be confused with a simple relativity of 'truths'. Truth changes in a *direction*, and it is not just the case that one view is as good as another. It was once 'true' that the world was square and became (more) true that it was round. What will be true of it in a thousand years is, obviously, impossible for us to say.

Nowhere is the necessity for courage and good faith more evident than in the search to establish the truth about relations between people, for in this process lies the threat of annihilation. As A struggles with B to lay bare the meaning of their conduct towards each other, bravely trying to stay clear of the slide into self-deception, to confess and accept his fear and vulnerability, to acknowledge his defensive strategies, his meannesses and malignancies and desperate cravings, so B can with a single act of bad faith betray the reciprocity of this process, perhaps by 'closing down' A with some kind of objectifying label which sends him spinning like a deflating balloon into the distant, icy, sterile reaches of isolation. For these reasons the exploration of subjective truth needs usually to be tentative, gentle, delicate; a process of negotiation which, to proceed satisfactorily, has first to construct a basis of trust. By its very nature, there are no rules which can be formulated for this procedure, since it takes place at, as it were, the very forefront of our conduct, involving our total, integrated effort; it leaves out no part of us which can sit back and conduct the proceedings self-consciously. There are some things, certainly, of which we should no doubt beware – for example, of self-justifying or comforting verbal constructions, of labels and diagnoses, but in the end it is only trust in one's subjective knowing that will inform us of success or failure. Many of the myth-creating properties of our everyday concepts could be avoided if we attended in our relations with each other to what we do rather than to what we say. In this way intuitive sensitivity deals with reality rather than with misleading verbal constructions of it. But this again cannot be turned into any kind of *method*, for method inevitably becomes once more a tool of objectivity.

It is, in fact, precisely the methodological dogma of objectivity which has to be rejected if we are to be able to acknowledge and pursue subjective truth. That is, we have to get used to the idea that we can do without – indeed to some extent *must* do without – the very things we have always understood to be indispensable for the reliable establishment of truth, if we are indeed to establish it. If it *suits* us, we may make use of the canons of reasoning or methods of quantification thought to be essential to science, but they can never on their own be enough to ensure a path to the truth, and may as often as not block it completely. But this does *not* mean that the end result of our search has no inter-subjective validity. In fact, the result of our negotiations concerning our subjective experience, where they have been successful, is a freely entered into commitment to the reality which we find we have in common.

Our culture makes it almost impossible to think of knowledge other than in terms of acquisition. Scientific knowledge, for example, is, especially in the current technological climate, treated almost exclusively as a kind of weapon, a powerful possession which we can use to subdue nature and add to our material well-being. We do *not* seem to use the knowledge we gain in this way so that *we may do things better*. Subjective knowledge may, on the' other hand, carry more this latter kind of implication – it contributes to part of a flowing process of conduct or activity which is not just about making use of things, but at least *may* be about how *we* may be useful. In this way, the knowledge which we achieve inter-subjectively does not *need*, as does scientific knowledge, to be fashioned into a monument to our own acquisitive cleverness, does not need to be spelt out articulately, studied academically, hoarded in books, appropriated by experts, but rather contributes, uncommented and uncommentable upon, to our efforts to fashion a world we cannot predict, but can only try to achieve. Such knowledge is to *some* extent safeguarded (though certainly not totally immune) from abuse precisely because it *cannot* be objectified and manipulated.

In pursuing the painful process of undeception there is no doubt a sense in which *self*-knowledge becomes important, but this, again, is not the kind of self-knowledge which most of us, I suspect, think will prove useful. It is all too easy to interpret the injunction 'know thyself' as a recommendation to become aware of that which one is in a kind of finished, objective way, so that one can, for example, put oneself to better use in the business of acquiring things while subduing the opposition. Knowing yourself, on this kind of view, means knowing yourself as an object which you can manipulate, knowing your strengths and weaknesses, knowing how to use yourself as a tool for getting what you want and keeping out of psychologically troublesome situations. Self-knowledge thus becomes yet another kind of 'skill' which marks its possessor as in some way superior to or more valuable than those who remain relatively ignorant of their 'selves'. There is no doubt that many psychological thinkers advocate this kind of objective self-knowledge as one of life's major goals, and it may puzzle many people to suggest that, because we do not 'possess' things like 'selves', it is not only undesirable to pursue knowledge of them, but the pursuit itself is doomed to failure. Claims to this kind of knowledge constitute the very essence of bad faith, since the one 'thing' that cannot be known is the subject who makes the claim. These, of course, are themes already met with in Chapter 3, but it still remains to clarify what *could* usefully be meant by 'self-knowledge'.

'Know thyself' might I think best be interpreted as a warning that one should, as part of a kind of continuous process of self-suspicion, keep a wary eye on what one is up to. This would *not* mean listening to the self-justifying accounts which we are always ready to tell ourselves, indeed it means specifically disregarding them, but rather attempting to divine from our own conduct what might be the nature of our undertakings. Unlike knowledge of self-as-object, this kind of process would never arrive at finite knowledge of any*thing* in particular, but would represent a kind of running battle not to fall into self-deception. This is not acquisitive knowledge, but knowledge which contributes to one's functioning in the world as a subjective influence within it; it keeps one in touch with reality. Again, one must frustrate the habitual objectivist urge to lay down a *method* whereby the pursuit of such knowing can be maintained – there is no certain method beyond the effort itself. It does seem however that, for example, patients who have begun through the process of negotiation in psychotherapy to see through their self-deceptive strategies do with practice often become better at recognizing what they are up to and learn to regard the stories they tell themselves with increasing scepticism. But if the threat is strong enough, if the painfulness of the world again becomes too much to contemplate, the slide back into self-deception is easily achieved.

To 'know yourself', then, involves a constant effort to maintain your integrity and honestly to acknowledge the projects which are revealed as the meaning of your conduct. There is no way of ensuring the success of this effort, and the knowledge which results from it is of no permanent use. No wonder, perhaps, that we are individually and collectively so reluctant to abandon the seductive promises of a much less personally demanding objectivity.

Slowly, then, we begin to find ourselves in a world without the familiar reference points supplied by objectivity, sharing knowledge which cannot be proved or put to use, losing the selves which we had always thought we had, discovering that even 'simply' knowing something demands of us the courage to take an active risk. But these are not new demands which are placed upon us, we are not required suddenly, like infants, to learn an entirely unfamiliar way of life, for all these are things which, to some extent at least, we have been doing all the time, though without taking account of them or taking them seriously. What happens, then, if we *trust* our subjective experience of ourselves and the world?

A number of 'humanistic' psychologies have extolled the virtues and benefits of being 'open to experience' as if the myths by which we live were *personal* creations which distort not only a clear, but in many respects a reassuring view of the world. Thus the implication is that openness to experience will somehow bring about a more personally rewarding life in which, free of the 'hang-ups' which we have somehow foolishly created for ourselves, we will see that the world is not such a bad place after all. The 'fully experiencing' person might be seen in these psychologies as likely to find as reward for his or her honesty, 'immediacy', etc., a 'deeply meaningful' relatedness to others in 'the here and now', a satisfactory flow of 'peak experiences', 'individuation', fulfilment, and a lot more besides.* Were this really the case, it would be difficult to understand why our objective mythology is maintained with such all-pervasive tenacity, since relinquishing it would appear to bring such easy benefits.

In fact, though there are no doubt liberating aspects in trusting one's own experience, there are many more which are painful, disturbing, and even terrifying. Objective mythology, as well as personal ('neurotic') self-deception, do not arise merely out of our having made a few silly mistakes about the nature of the world or ourselves – they protect us from a vista we can hardly bear to behold. However, the price we pay for self-deception, for too eagerly grabbing the opportunity our linguistic capacity gives us for misrepresenting our reality, is in the long run likely to be greater than the pain and panic afforded by subjective insight. Personal self-deception is likely to lead to confusion and anxiety upon which the individual can simply gain no purchase, and collective mythology is maintained at the expense of the gradual disintegration of the social world and the physical environment. It is only as subjects that we can influence or alter anything, and it is only by taking the risks involved in acknowledging our subjectivity that we can hope to improve our condition. The point of acknowledging subjectivity is not to achieve 'fulfilment', but to be able to act upon the world.

It is true, I think, that people may experience a sense of relief in admitting to themselves a vision of their reality that they had fought to deny. The 'agoraphobic' housewife, for example,

* R. D. Rosen, in *Psychobabble*, Avon Books, 1979, has exposed the shallowness of several of these approaches to psychological well-being.

who is able eventually to acknowledge, say, her loneliness and insecurity, her anger at her husband, her occasional murderous rage towards her children, at least no longer needs to pretend that her distress arises from mysterious sources beyond her experience; she is no longer a passive victim of the inexplicable, though she does of course find herself in a world full of real difficulties. Breaking free of myth may also allow one a refreshing appreciation of *meaning* – the wordless fears, unpleasant physical sensations, the 'symptoms', the uneasy and inarticulate preoccupations and forebodings which, perhaps, overshadowed daily existence, suddenly become linked to actual experience, pointing, as it were, to something out in the world (a situation, perhaps, or a relationship) which is an intelligible source of distress. People who permit themselves to acknowledge the significance of what they are subjectively, bodily informed of, are suddenly able to believe what they have always tried not to know, and if nothing else that tends to clear up a good deal of confusion.

Clarity, however, brings with it a series of further difficulties which may seem almost insuperably daunting. These involve not only the disturbing nature of what is revealed about the world, but also the consequences of being prepared to acknowledge that things may not be quite as one had thought.

Most of us withdraw confidence from our subjective experience of the social world at a fairly early age once it becomes apparent that relations with others are fraught with danger. To keep track of the truth of what is passing between oneself and others is both intensely threatening and very complex, especially as it demands the kind of sceptical attitude towards one's own stance which is necessitated by the untrustworthiness of what one tells oneself. Worst of all, recognition of the threats, demands, embargoes, pleas, severances and dependencies, hopes and fears we place upon each other, puts us in a position where we feel almost impelled to *do* something about aspects of relationships which can no longer be ignored. Recognizing what is the case leaves one suddenly unsupported by the myths which maintain a comfortable blindness. The married woman, for example, who finally admits to herself that she no longer has the unqualified support which she had thought to be the meaning of her husband's love, that in fact he needs her to provide him with a kind of unstinted mothering of which she feels simply incapable, who begins to see that behind the apparent mutuality of their courting days and early married life there lurks the separateness of two people whose experience leads them to widely differing expectations of human relationships, who begins to see, perhaps, that she originally married her husband as an escape from a particularly uncomfortable relationship with her father – this woman is faced with some very disturbing possibilities indeed, and is thrown into a region of uncertainty in her personal life for which our culture provides almost no signposts. Is, for example, her situation unusual? Does she leave her husband in the confident expectation that, with hindsight and more mature judgment, she can make a happier and more suitable relationship? Does she, on the other hand, conclude that her situation is the rule rather than the exception, and that her insight into it in fact gives her a better than average chance of being able to work for its betterment? Our objective culture operates precisely to obscure from our view what goes on in our own lives, and hence offers us no help when we start to discover for ourselves the nature of our predicament.

Those people who opt for a self-deceptive strategy for avoiding this kind of discovery may do so partly out of a dimly sensed anticipation that to acknowledge what in their heart they know to be the case would be to bring about catastrophe. To draw attention to the emperor's nakedness is to initiate the collapse of the entire social system. Or so one may fear. Part of the feeling of relief with which people find that their 'symptoms' are in fact indications of a state of affairs that they had formerly not dared to recognize is probably due to their realizing that no catastrophe has taken place, however daunting the need to act upon their insights might be. The objective (for example, 'illness') view is often maintained through a kind of blackmail which conjures up a superstitious terror in those who even contemplate calling its bluff. The child who innocently threatens to expose the secrets of its parents' vulnerability is likely to experience the full blast of this reign of terror in its original and most powerful form. For adults, however, acknowledgment of the subjective truth is not often met by the disaster they expect in imagination.

There is no doubt that to be honest with oneself is to recognize a terrible vulnerability and to see that there is no escape from the risks which involvement with the world entails. One can never become a safe success, never, without monumental self-deception, bask in the security of having become the satisfactory object of everybody's esteem. Every new enterprise, every new relationship carries with it the possibility of failure; nothing is guaranteed. As a subject, one is, as it were, inescapably dedicated to living out the meaning of one's own ineradicable experience. We of course differ from each other in terms of the content of that experience, though our manner of experiencing may be very similar – more similar, as I have argued, than we are usually prepared to admit. He whose parents nurtured his early years with wise and loving concern is likely to have more confidence in himself and others than she whose father subjected her in her first ten years to an unremitting sadistic battering. Each is likely to draw different lessons from experience, and to pursue different projects. There is a loneliness about this which is very hard for most of us to take. How much easier it would be to be a standardized unit in a vast impersonal machine!

There is an added complication to a belated trust in one's own experience, to acknowledging, say, that one is not the passive victim of an illness ('anxiety state') but rather the vulnerable contributor to a network of complicated and dangerous relationships. For in making any such acknowledgment, which entails beginning to take responsibility for those aspects of one's own conduct which contribute to one's predicament, it becomes immediately apparent that time formerly spent in self-deception was *wasted* time. Admitting that one was wrong, even over trivial matters, is never a particularly comfortable experience; admitting that one has made life-long mistakes and entertained entirely misleading assumptions about matters of vital personal importance is all the more painful, and constitutes often a major stumbling block to the development of a more accurate perception of the meaning of one's conduct.

It helps with the *painfulness* of honesty to extend to oneself the same kind of compassion one would extend to others. Many people confronting for the first time what they see as their own futility and contemptible vulnerability, realizing with a rush of shame the cowardliness of their self-deception, are comforted a little by the suggestion that they should look at themselves as if they were someone else, and remember that the world they live in gave them good reasons for doing what they did. Having reasons, furthermore, is not the same as being to blame or being at fault. The self-disgust of the shy man who begins to see that he is afraid of people rather than 'ill' does not usually constitute the kind of feeling he would see as applicable to other shy people, and it may in fact be possible for him to regard himself with the same kind of reassuring warmth that he would want to offer them.

However, whatever crumbs of comfort may be gleaned from breaking free of objective mythology, the immediate consequences seem not at first sight devoutly to be wished. Among other things, thus, the person finds him- or herself vulnerably adrift with no more guidance than his or her own convictions in a world full of pain and danger, isolated in a standpoint which most seem unwilling to share, and faced with having to do something about it. It is hardly surprising that in these circumstances most of us would feel that we can scarcely be expected to cope.

# 9   The Confrontation of Reality

There is no doubt that, in facing life's difficulties, it helps to be loved. When the gaze of the Other becomes warm and approving, when we are confirmed as good, or as beautiful, the freezing winds of isolation and despair give way to a glowing self-confidence, a kind of amniotic security which, perhaps, formed the basis of some of our very earliest experiences, and which, again perhaps, we may have been seeking to recreate ever since.

It is scarcely possible, however, to conceive of love in our own time as anything but conditional and 'object-directed'. Love is both our salvation and our greatest danger: he or she who loves reciprocally and without defences takes the most terrifying risk of annihilation. Love confirms you as a satisfactory object, but its withdrawal may destroy you. Whether or not you are loved is likely to depend on your behaving in accordance with your lover's needs and expectations. Lovers must watch each other warily, fake, dissemble, and be ready at a moment's notice to defend themselves.

To be relatively confident and free of the tortures of self-doubt and self-disgust, it helps to have been loved as a child – usually, of course, this means to have had loving parents, i.e. parents who approved of and took an interest in you. Again, in sexual and marital relationships, it helps if the partners like and appreciate each other, take a real interest in each other, confirm each other's embodied presence in the world (it helps if they find each other beautiful and desirable). Being loved helps so much, in fact, that we try to establish it at the very centre of our interpersonal culture, so to speak. Love is all; all you need is love. We proclaim the importance of love, we hold 'love-ins', we sing about it and dream about it and advocate it as the only possible basis for marriage and family life. We see the desperate need for it so clearly that we pretend love we cannot feel, we attach ourselves to eviscerated religions in which we lie hysterically to each other about the extent of our mutual loving. We turn love into a commodity which can be bought and sold. We lie and cheat for love, we steal and extort it, for only love assuages the lonely terror of empty objectivity. You are nothing if you are not loved.

It helps to be loved, but not many people are. Hence, no doubt, our concern to increase the supply of love, to professionalize

its provision and advocate its universal desirability. But
we fail to see that this is the conditional love of the market
economy. As objects, we are victims of the laws of supply and
demand. Love, like gold, must be scarce if it is to retain the
meaning we give it. It must be competed for, and there will be
many losers. There are, certainly, those who are rich in love,
and who consequently are happy, but it is as realistic to aim for
a society made up of such individuals as it would be to aim for a
society composed only of millionaires. Those who have been
deprived of love, but get, as it were, a sudden windfall, may well
find that the tenor of their lives changes from dull, aching
self-hatred to undreamed-of joy. The supply of love is not equit-
able or even; unfairly, like money, it can probably he inherited.

Love is not to be sneezed at. In a society in which we have all
become objects, it is the best and most fulfilling mode in which
to conduct our relations with each other. Love and happiness go
hand-in-hand. Love protects us from the sheer brutal savagery
otherwise so apparent in our social intercourse. Love is our
emotional currency, without which we cannot, it seems, exist.

I do not wish to disparage love, indeed I am sure that we
*should* be loving towards each other, but I do think that, in
allowing love to have become inextricably enmeshed with the
values of objectivity we have created a threat (the withdrawal
of love) which, combined with the fact that there can never be
enough love to go around, forces us to defend ourselves with
such desperation that we become almost incapable of conduct-
ing our lives sanely and safely. We stand in danger of making
love indispensable to our survival. That would be fine if there
*were* enough of it to go around, but there isn't. Not even by
buying and selling love on a vast scale, not even by faking and
fabricating it on every side, will we be able to meet the need for
it which we have created. Most people most of the time are
facing a difficult and frightening world with only very little if
any at all of the protection afforded by love, and the only other
ways in which they can survive involve the pretence that
things are not as bad as they know they are. Love is at the
same time our highest salvation and our greatest myth, and it
is mythical to the extent that we see it as the answer to our
'problems'.

Apart from straightforward self-deception, which has
perhaps by now received enough attention in this book, there
are a number of other answers, not depending solely upon the
acquisition of love, which our culture allows for the attempted

solution of the problems it poses us.

Because individual, personal adequacy plays so central a part in determining a person's worth, to self as well as to others, it is not surprising that the cultivation of adequacy – or indeed of *in*adequacy – may become the ruling preoccupation of our lives. Here again it is the individual self-as-object which is the focus of attention. How adequate we may feel ourselves to be depends on the extent to which we have achieved personal happiness and fulfilment through material success and satisfactory 'relationships'. Our psychological as well as our material goals are defined in terms of acquisition rather than instrumentality – i.e., what we 'end up as' is considered much more important than what we do.* Though we may pay lip-service to half-remembered religious precepts such as 'by their works ye shall know them', we are for the most part utterly impervious to the moral intention or significance of our conduct, and on the whole what we do is evaluated mainly in terms of what it achieves for the enhancement of our image and the augmentation of our power, status and material advantage. It would be hard for us to conceive of a life as being fulfilled or successful unless it terminated in a roseate glow of comfort and love, material well-being and social respect. It seems to us at the very least somehow unfair that Christ should have died on the cross, that Mozart should have been buried unidentifiably in a pauper's grave, or that Tolstoy should have breathed his last at a tiny provincial railway station amid the chaotic and bitter emotional turmoil of his family relations. Not that we have to look to such exalted regions to find evidence that life is not as we should like it to be. It is virtually only the mythified diet of 'fact' and fiction fed to us by the 'entertainment media', the reassuring pomp and circumstance of the occasional state funeral, which prop up the 'credibility' of our cherished ideals. The truth is to be found near at hand in hospital wards, old people's homes, and indeed within our own families. The happiness and fulfilment upon which we suppose the meaning of our lives to depend in fact constitute an illusion to which our collective cowardice in the face of the truth leads us to hang on desperately even though for each of us in our individual experience it is an illusion which is shattered over and over again. Of course there is a tiny minority which does appear to achieve the goals so assiduously pursued by the rest of us, but their success

* This, of course, is the central theme of E. Fromm's book, *To Have or to Be*, Jonathan Cape, 1978.

*depends upon* our failure. All this is only a cause for despair if we are incapable of conceiving the meaning of our existence in anything other than individual and objective terms. Though it may be frightening to penetrate the myth, to do so may be preferable to spending an entire lifetime in fruitless pursuit of mythical goals.

After all, what is one supposed to do with, for example, 'fulfilment' and 'deeply meaningful' relationships? The cultivation of self, the acquisition of confidence and self-esteem, the occupation of a central point in a network of warm and loving relationships, the final, if brief, satisfaction of having rounded off one's life in the achievement of all one's major aims – is it really self-evident that these are the best goals we can imagine for ourselves? Most psychologies which are concerned with anything more than the relief of 'symptoms' do seem to suggest that there can be no more desirable outcome to a life than the achievement of some such *personal* satisfaction. The fact that nobody ever actually achieves it does not seem to deter us from continuing to pursue it or from persuading ourselves of its desirability; nor do we notice that our failure to achieve it leaves us more and more confused and desperate. The psychological and spiritual problems we set ourselves (in regard to 'fulfilment', 'individuation', etc.) share all the banality of that presented by our material acquisitiveness: what do you do when the novelty of the new car wears off?

There are, of course, those who recognize quite early on that they are doomed to lose in the race for fulfilment, and see no alternative but to carve out for themselves a career in the cultivation of inadequacy. The painfulness of trying when you are virtually certain you will fail should not be underestimated: one cannot live perpetually with the shattering anticipation of disaster without eventually simply falling apart, and in these circumstances it is almost with relief that one can opt for failure. Indeed, the role of failed, inadequate object can become so (relatively) comfortable that people may hang on to it very tenaciously even when life offers them a sudden unexpected opportunity. The young woman who has accepted a definition of herself as ugly, fat and bad and pursues a series of degrading relationships with men who treat her with callous indifference and contempt may actually turn down the attentions of a concerned, gentle and attractive lover partly because she simply cannot bear the potentiality for hurt in the hopes which start to stir within her. The man who has always seemed to stake his self-esteem on getting promotion at work, perhaps resentfully pointing out the inferiority of others who seem unfairly to have beaten him to it, may suddenly succumb to a host of debilitating and mysterious 'symptoms' when he is himself unexpectedly offered the promotion he always coveted. Fake martyrdom is a far more attractive role than most of us like to think: it appears morally unassailable, and it carries no risks. For the price of a little suffering (which with luck may have the advantage of drawing some sympathy from others), one may live quite safe from the awful threat of annihilation which is incurred by taking risks. In real life Cinderella will continue to scrub the floor on her knees even when nobody is standing over her, will develop an immobilizing illness on the day of the ball, and will in any case disclaim vehemently any suggestion that the slipper is her size.

There is of course much more to this kind of phenomenon than simple cowardice: as I have argued earlier, we cannot just erase our early experience, but most likely spend our lives doggedly pursuing its significance in every aspect. Contrary to what many people, including many psychologists and psychiatrists, seem to think, we cannot slip from role to role, even with the most massive amounts of help. Our language, literature and drama can project for us infinitely variable 'realities' and modes of being; we can so easily *think* of being different that we may be forgiven for supposing that actual change is really not all that difficult to achieve. But it is perhaps precisely because our experience, and our conduct in relation to it, are so concrete and resistant to manipulation that we are so fascinated by the fantastic possibilities offered by language. Those of us who offer professionally to change lives and alter experience are in this aspect little more than conjurors paid to reinforce some of our culture's more comforting myths.

Most of us, I suspect, live our lives bewildered by the pain in which we find ourselves, discovering over and over again that our actual experiences – whether concerning childhood, work, love, marriage, parenthood, old age, death – fall far short of those our mythology leads us to anticipate, or at least hope for. Desperately we may try to shut out our recognition of reality, smile through our despair, by becoming enthusiastic mythologizers ourselves. And despair and isolation increase in direct proportion to the fatuity of our myths. Those who have been stamped 'reject' early on – and one wonders whether they may not be a majority – live lives, if not tortured, then haunted by a kind of hopeless, aching pain which never seems to be assuaged for long, and which, even if expressible, is hardly ever expressed because our mythology does not permit its recognition. One's 'inadequacy' can be experienced as a dreadful secret which may suddenly be exposed at any time; 'anxiety' often stems from a sense of the imminence of such exposure.

Another apparent way out of the dilemmas posed by our existence as objects in a threatening world is to attempt to preserve indefinitely that state in which we felt most safe – i.e., infancy or childhood. The responsibility and isolation of adulthood are things very few of us manage to accept, and in view of our early experience of dependency and protection, this is hardly surprising. The hierarchical and fundamentally authoritarian nature of almost all our social and political organizations reflects our continued need for parental supervision. However resentfully and vociferously we may demand independence, it is usually the last thing we really want, and we may actually find it terrifying. To find oneself as an adult in an adult world is rather like waking as a child unexpectedly to find the house on fire and only one's brothers and sisters on the premises. How can one organize, cooperate, take responsibility, decide what to do, without a parent (leader) to point the way and keep the others under control? Those politicians, I suspect, who appeal to the electorate, even if patronizingly, as parents who know best start with an enormous psychological advantage over those who address us as brothers, sisters or comrades – who would trust the running of the country to their brothers and sisters? It is a tragedy built into the very structure of our experience that we must eventually perform the function of adults while feeling like children, and it is no surprise that we may try to escape the conflict involved by offering our childish allegiance to some mythified person, social structure or idea which represents Authority. We may also reject our own adult status by refusing to exercise the authority which inevitably falls to us, for example in bringing up children.

It is part of objective culture to reinforce the idea that on almost every question of factual or moral importance there are others (experts, professionals) who 'know best', and in this respect objectivity plays straight into our need for parental reassurance and escape from adult responsibility. One of the most threatening things to be experienced by many people is to be called upon suddenly for an opinion, especially in the presence of a judging Other, for in being asked without warning to take up a stance the possibility of exposure of one's inadequacy is increased a thousandfold. But objects do not make judgments, and 'science' is value-free and therefore ethically neutral. The 'scientist's' spiritual parent is the methodological dogma to which he or she subscribes, and association with scientific culture therefore frees one from some of the uncomfortable features attached to being an adult person.

The only hope of our recognizing the truth of our predicament, becoming a part of as well as being able to influence our reality, lies, I believe, in our making the transition from object to subject. For most of us this is a far from painless process, and many never even dream of its possibility. Paradoxically, it is in our 'symptoms' of anxiety, distress and malaise that encouraging signs are to be found of the insistence of the subject on being recognized. It is thus in our capacity to be disturbed by the false objectivity of our world that the greatest hope lies for our being able to do something about it.

Many patients talk with puzzled longing of the days when they felt 'all right'. People who feel that their confidence and ability to cope have utterly ebbed away may remember nostalgically a time when they could do anything and go anywhere. Many interpret this as an indication that something has 'gone wrong' in a way which could in principle be mechanically repaired. On the whole, however, it seems more likely that the myths and distractions they were able to live by can no longer disguise the gravity of their predicament; the accuracy of a subjective view, breaking through as panic or dread, can no longer be denied. To make proper use of the opportunities opened up by the acknowledgment of distress is to take one of the few paths open to us to develop and assert our subjectivity. It is those for whom the myths are not working, the 'unsuccessful' and painfully self-conscious (as opposed to the successful image-makers) who, paradoxically perhaps, stand one of the better chances of becoming aware of the real world around them. Psychological distress and anxiety are thus not indications of illness or abnormality, but the inevitable experiences of anyone who begins to become aware, however dimly, of the disparity between myth and reality. Our culture, it is true, offers them almost no hope at all of understanding their experience, but even so their experience is more a sign of the culture's failure than of theirs. I do not mean to romanticize or ennoble suffering – there are enough 'martyrs' as it is – but only to emphasize that there is a *meaning* to our misery, and one which we may take note of. Again, this meaning need not be one we have to spell out laboriously in words: as always, it is only the literal-minded objectivist who insists on being able to *say* what things mean. As with our dreams, for example, our despair, our sense of dread or our 'symptoms' may move us and have significance for us in ways which we cannot articulate but which nevertheless alter quite profoundly our stance towards the world.

I do not wish to suggest that the experience of psychological distress and anxiety is *necessary* for the transition from object to subject. Those who remain true throughout their lives to the significance of their personal experience (the reality revealed by their intuitive sensitivity) may never experience anything like a 'symptom' of the kind which stems from failing self-deception, but nor will they be likely to find life comfortable. The gradual falling away of myth, the process of becoming adult from infant, of travelling from birth to death with one's eyes open may involve a continual (and literal) process of dis-illusionment as agonizing as having the skin slowly stripped from one's body. This, again, is only really a problem if one regards one's personal comfort, 'fulfilment', etc., as particularly important. One may instead be distracted from these latter concerns by attending to the effectiveness of what one does. This is not asking for any special saintliness – there are many people who unself-consciously live out a life of absorption in activity without ever realizing, or needing to realize, that this is what they are doing.

What happens, then, to the person who, by whatever route, comes to discover that, contrary to all previous expectations, he or she is a subject rather than an object?

The world which is revealed to the subjective gaze is in almost all aspects the opposite of how it seemed under the rule of objectivity, and to confront it unflinchingly may at first be a vertiginously frightening experience. Where before one had a defined role in an articulated social structure which operated largely automatically and mechanically, where one was more or less literally a cog in the machine, suddenly now one finds oneself in a fluid, evolving world full of untagged, unarticulated meaning, in which one's own conduct may alter the course of events in unpredictable ways, in which one has no feeling for what kind of an object one is, and which seems to present undreamed-of threats and dangers. To catch such a glimpse of reality is enough to send some people into a kind of perpetual frenzy of anxiety in which they insist on the validity of myth to the point of resorting to the basest emotional blackmail of anyone around them who threatens to blow the gaff. Not only may people in this state drive their children crazy through their insistence on a false reality of their own construction, but they may even succeed in establishing myths which generalize beyond those immediately closest to them. I suspect, for example, that the phenomenon 'poltergeist' has in some instances gained credibility only through the ability of one member of a family who has succumbed to personally unacknowledgeable violent rage to terrorize the rest into silence and pretended ignorance concerning the havoc that has been wrought. In any case, one is unwise to underestimate the lengths to which people may go to hide from themselves and others the unpalatable truth. However, such extreme reactions to the sight of reality are the exception rather than the rule.

People I know who have through a long process of negotiation been able to edge their way into acceptance of their own subjectivity are often indignant at their inability to be able to deal immediately with what they find. Our existence as the passively consuming termini of a huge nurturing machine, our lifetime of experience of being trained but not learning, being acted upon but not acting, being chosen but not choosing, ill prepares us for the new terrain in which we find ourselves. To the object newly become subject it seems almost an outrage to be placed in unfamiliar territory without a map. Sometimes it helps people in this circumstance to think of their task as analogous to that of the explorers of old, who presumably did not depart for darkest Africa expecting to recognize the landscape when they got there. If, say, you have spent the last three decades thinking of yourself as the worthless victim of fate in a world which is otherwise populated by happy and effective people who will only look upon you with pity or disgust, it is not easy to know how you set about your relations with them once you have realized that you are as much Other for them as they are for you. How do you cope when you realize that your 'illness' was despair, or rage, or hatred, or longing or confusion? How do you calm your terror at finding yourself the centre of a network of relationships which does in fact reverberate to *your* conduct? Suddenly you are faced with the reality of concepts which objectivity had promised to render obsolete. Concepts, that is, like courage, loneliness, difficulty, uncertainty, faith. Learning becomes slow, painful and risky, the conduct of relationships delicate and dangerous, the future in principle unpredictable. At times like these the allure of hypnotism or electric shock is not hard to understand.

To find oneself a subjective adult rather than an objective infant, to do without the comforting myths which seemed to point the path along which one could be ushered through life, to take responsibility for what one does knowing that the outcome of one's conduct is uncertain is likely at first to be experienced, by those who are able to face it at all, as that kind of pain which is often called 'depression'. To be uprooted, isolated, confused and uncertain is a physical experience the meaning of which is clear enough to a subjective view, though its clarity makes it none the more pleasant. For many people in this position, life for a while becomes a kind of Pilgrim's Progress in which they stumble from despondency to terror as unfamiliarity and directionlessness are replaced by unknown obstacles looming unanticipated round the turn of a corner.

There is no doubt that one needs courage – and wherever possible encouragement – to pursue this course, and that courage can probably only be summoned up in the context of faith, i.e. faith that somehow what one is trying to do is worth doing. Objectivity, of course, attempts to replace faith with certainty through the exercise of 'scientific prediction and control'. But since we ourselves are, through our conduct, determiners of our world and our fate, and since we cannot know ourselves and each other as fully analysable and therefore completely understandable objects, we are in reality doomed to operate without certainty. Our conduct is inevitably uncertain precisely because we are not, and cannot be, machines, and it is this uncertainty and unpredictability which in large part constitutes the *moral* nature of our conduct. We are absolutely unavoidably faced over and over again with having to do what we think is right rather than what we know will be effective, and the more we try to hide this truth from ourselves the more blind, and probably destructive, will our influence on the world actually become.

It is not inconceivable that in the course of progressing with the pilgrimage of newly discovered subjectivity initial fear and despair may give way to something more like elation as the realization dawns that one is not an object labelled, anchored and evaluated for all time, but rather a freely flowing focus of action through which one may to *some* extent take charge of one's own fate. At the very least, having recognized that *in fact* the way courses of events become altered is through the intervention of people, one might hope to bring one's subjective influence to bear on those courses of events with which one is directly engaged and which formerly seemed objectively unalterable. This is not the same as saying, as some 'humanistic' psychologies do, that the subject can become *anything* he or she wants, or do anything he or she likes. Indeed, subjects may have to recognize and take responsibility for a quite narrow line of conduct which is likely to bring them little personal satisfaction or happiness. As always, one must beware of confusing the projects and possibilities which one can construct in words with those in which one is actually engaged. Reality lies in what we do, not in what we tell ourselves, and what we do arises, often, out of our passionate (even if tacit) commitment to the lessons of our experience. The nature of that commitment does not necessarily change just through our being able to put it into words and imagine it otherwise.

People who see the possibility of taking some kind of subjective charge of their lives will not be able simply to erase their previously painful experience, and learning new ways of responding to circumstances or people with whom they find themselves in a new, probably more responsible, relationship, will not be easy. The whole message of the professionalized management of human relations and 'problems' such as that found in psychiatry and psychology is of relative ease, passivity and painlessness, and so most people are not expecting to encounter the degree of difficulty in learning to conduct themselves in this kind of sphere that they might consider reasonable enough were they trying to acquire competence in, say, a particular sport, craft or art. For example, a patient who gets to the point where she is determined to 'take on' her shyness, suddenly baulks at going to a small social gathering because she realizes that she does not 'know what to do'. There are two aspects to her difficulty, one being a mistaken assumption that other people *do* know what to do (i.e., that they have some kind of prepared map for how the evening will go), but the other a more reasonable sense of her own lack of practice in such situations. Even in this latter respect, having pursued a fairly conventional existence in the world for thirty-five years, she is more competent than she thinks she is, but she has always defined herself as utterly worthless and incapable. Ultimately she will only gain in confidence through risking herself in threatening situations and discovering thereby that no catastrophe of major proportions results. Just as sportsmen or artists could never acquire competence without its becoming built into their bodies through practice, so experience of situations or events that used, probably out of fear, to be shunned, just must now be physically acquired if the fear is to be overcome. Even learning to play the piano demands a degree of courage the necessity for which may be avoided by listening instead to the hifi.

The avoidance of *difficulty* has become a kind of imperative in our age of passive objectivity. We take it as a self-evident technological (invertedly moral) axiom that 'less difficult' equals 'preferable'. To say that a course of action is 'difficult' is to condemn it as inferior or unworkable, to offer a seemingly unchallengeable objection to it. From the subjective viewpoint such a stance is utterly fallacious: the bodily engagement of the subject with the world is inescapably difficult, if only because of the at least mildly painful adjustment to its demands that the world exacts from the body. In precisely this way learning the piano is for most people, among other things, a painful experience. Not only does one have a heart-sinking awareness of the steadily increasing complexity of the task before one (which makes the mastery of a five-finger exercise, once it has been achieved, seem absolutely paltry), but the sheer physical frustration of trying to discipline one's fingers to conform to the unnatural dictates of the keys while having to coordinate this with the maddeningly abstract significance of the musical notation, is a seemingly endlessly repeated challenge to one's capacity for self-imposed torture. Why should facing and, as far as possible, learning to deal with the complexities and difficulties of one's personal world be any easier? Just as the child sits before the piano weeping with frustration and screaming 'I can't do it', so people who emerge from a fog of self-deception to find themselves beset by absolutely concrete tasks 'out there' in the world, fall back in horror at their initial incompetence to take them on. But it is equally as unreasonable for them to *expect* to be competent as it is for the child to expect to be able to play the piano without having learned. Again, the fusion of 'science' and magic in our culture frequently makes the validity of this argument almost impossible to maintain: over and over again people will be seduced by the blandishments of those 'experts' who offer easy solutions to the 'problems' which in actuality necessitate painful bodily involvement with the world. So out of touch with our reality have we become that, for example, many people find reasonably plausible the idea that one could while asleep learn a foreign language 'subliminally' from a tape-recorder under one's pillow.

Perhaps the most difficult myth of all to give up is the myth of togetherness. Although there is much that is subjective which can become inter-subjective, there is almost certainly some that isn't, and in any case the more that one departs from the tenets of popular mythology the more isolated one becomes. Whoever dares comment on the emperor's nakedness is likely to become part of a very small minority indeed, and one which provokes the hostility and derision of the majority. Furthermore, if we find ourselves unable to conduct our lives and understand our experience in accordance with the utterly banal precepts and expectations provided by our mythology, we are likely to find the almost total absence of any more helpful source of wisdom doubly disconcerting: in the entirely unexpected set of circumstances in which we find ourselves there is no one to tell us what to do, and no body of knowledge readily to hand to reassure us that we are not alone in our predicament. The emperor's nakedness is a discovery which can only be made personally and individually; imperial schools and libraries will be concerned only to suppress recognition of this phenomenon. Hard to bear though this isolation may be, it does have the advantage of conferring upon those who experience it the dignity of being human and the possibility of making some kind of personal contribution to the moral evolution of the species. As mechanized units we are safe in that we need not ever individually stick our necks out, but we are also expendable and interchangeable, condemned to eternal objectivity; we may be programmed, but we may never expect to programme. But in so far as the unique aspects of our experience force us into areas of exploration where, so it seems, nobody else has been, we may at least hope that our discoveries may be of help or illumination to others who find themselves in the same kind of isolation. We can make as well as follow maps.

Some aspects of the discomfort of subjectivity may be directly related to the extent to which one is still unable to abandon one's needs as object, and it seems unlikely that anyone could ever abandon these entirely. Because self-consciousness entails becoming the object of one's own awareness, to be completely subjective would be, among other things, to be completely unself-conscious, and any such being is hard to imagine, though no doubt there are some people who come close. As soon as one becomes aware of oneself as under the gaze of the Other, even where the Other is oneself, awareness of one's objective shortcomings gives rise to pain. Utter selfless absorption in some kind of active, bodily engagement with the world excludes experience of the kind of psychological distress which has been the focus of this book. Small children totally taken up with what they are doing – no doubt in part because they have no words to represent themselves to themselves – can be touchingly unaware of the extent to which they are exposed to the mockery of an observer (though, of course, what in adults we would see as absurd, in them we see as sweet). People absorbed in the performance of an art or a craft may be utterly free of the pain which floods back once their awareness of their 'selves' returns.

The subjective person is concerned not with being (anything in particular) but with doing. *People* are not to be evaluated, but their *deeds* may be. What one does at a particular point does not at *any* point define what one is – for example, one might make music without 'being a musician'. In relation to other subjects the subjective person pursues his or her activities in what Roger Poole calls 'ethical space':* what we do to and with each other becomes part of an ever-evolving moral process in which there is no objective guarantee of prediction or control.

Since everything about our culture tends towards turning people into objects and estranging them from their own conduct and activity, what you do is of almost no significance alongside the importance of what you are, and in any case what you do can probably be done better by real machines. To attempt to up-end these values by laying on subjectivity the emphasis we now lay on objectivity would seem on the face of it to be almost insanely utopian (and would, incidentally, no doubt also undermine the social, cultural and economic foundations of our way of life far more radically than any merely political revolution). And yet, paradoxically, to acknowledge our subjectivity is doing no more than acknowledging what is already the case: *in fact* what evolves our world and seals our fate is nothing other than our own activity. This is even more true of our collective activity than it is of the self-deceiving, 'neurotic' activity of individuals, since the causes of their distress more often lie outside their control. Where we act in bad faith, in the collec-

* Roger Poole, *Towards Deep Subjectivity*, Allen Lane, The Penguin Press, 1972.

tive as in the individual case, the authorship of our actions is denied, and we become the helpless objects of what is in fact our own conduct. To free ourselves of the illusion of objectivity is therefore as much an acknowledgment of truth as a merely utopian gesture.

Were we able to live our lives focusing only on the value of what we did, unaware of ourselves as certain kinds of objects in the eyes of other people, engaged bodily with the world in order to realize our projects within it, relating to each other in 'ethical space' rather than in terms of an objective struggle for relative power or status, we should be unlikely to be suffering the kinds of psychological malaise to which our current society gives rise. The opportunities given us by language to misrepresent the meaning of our conduct to both ourselves and others no doubt renders impossible the attainment of a subjective social world in anything like pure culture. It would be absurd to suppose that we could use language solely in the 'vernacular' mode discussed by Ivan Illich* – i.e., as facilitating unself-conscious cooperation in the course of doing or making things together – and one must no doubt resign oneself to the fact that the capacity of human beings to posture before a linguistic mirror in which they can excite their greed and self-importance with all kinds of insubstantial images of greatness will never allow them to develop the kind of business-like sobriety with which animals not possessed of language conduct their lives. Nevertheless, it may be of some comfort to those whose very distress allows them to glimpse the falsity of our objective values to realize that in fact they *can* do things, and indeed that there may be some things worth doing.

There are some very tangible benefits to the acceptance of subjective as opposed to objective values. For example, in a world in which doing was valued over being, those millions of people who now live in more or less continuous pain and shame over the size and shape of their bodies would suddenly find that that issue simply became irrelevant. In the 'being world' the body is an object in competition for approval with other objects; in the 'doing-world' the body becomes an instrument, and while the effectiveness with which it achieves its aims may come under scrutiny from time to time, its physical properties are of scant interest. This again is no mere utopian ideal – in fact, of course, despite the objective bias of our aesthetics, beauty *is*

* I. Illich, *Shadow Work*, Marion Boyars, 1981.

conferred by the loving or appreciative eye of the beholder. Though even in the most rarefied areas of our cultural development we are not free of the polluting influence of objectification (in classical ballet even the most sublimely gifted dancer will be rejected if she departs by an inch from the standard mould), it is still the case that the experience of beauty in another person, if it is to be more than a fleeting, split-off acquisitive interest, arises from the relation *between* people. Whether or not people experience or are experienced by each other as beautiful depends on what they do in relation to each other and to the world, and in this respect it is the very individuality of the person's body which the other experiences as beautiful – not its conformity to a standardized cultural norm of some kind. Unfortunately, the fact that this is a truism does not prevent people from trying desperately to achieve a mythical objective standard of beauty, and feeling hopeless misery when, as inevitably they must, they fall short of it.

Even love itself is transformed in a world imbued by subjective values, for it ceases to constitute the bestowal of approval or confirmation upon a person-as-object, and becomes instead the facilitation of a person's embodied activity. By the latter I do not mean some kind of bloodlessly distant engineering of the person's environment, but rather the kind of loving attention some gardeners might give to the contents of their gardens, as opposed to, say, the acquisitive pride some collectors of art or antiques might have for the items in their collection. Subjective love involves the loving subject in the active taking of risks of a kind which are particularly threatening and repugnant to those who place their faith in objective being, since they necessitate taking a stance and making judgments which depend on little more than the individual's personal assessment and intuition of the concerns, possibilities and needs of the loved person. One can see the operation, or indeed the lack, of this kind of active loving particularly clearly in situations where one person or group of people is responsible for the care of another person or number of people. Subjectively loving parents, for example, watch their children's conduct with an attentive eye, not judging them as objects, but identifying and where possible encouraging and facilitating the nature and extent of their engagement with the world. In practice this might among other things mean, for example, noticing and nurturing their children's interests, competences and passions, using their greater power and experience as adults to clear space for and remove obstacles in the way of their children's own development as subjectively active beings. In this way parents may place all their resources at the disposal of their children, so that the latter may actively use them in their personal understanding and elaboration of the world. This involves a collaborative effort, a fusion; not a standing-back.

To attempt, as many people seem to do, not to 'influence' children morally for fear of impeding their growth is as foolish as it would be not to speak English to them for fear of biasing their linguistic development; parents cannot escape passing on a culture and adopting a range of attitudes towards the world, but this does not mean that they have to be punitively moralistic or unnecessarily constraining of their children's possibilities for developing different understandings. Of course a gardener might insist that marrows should be raised like radishes, and if he does no doubt they will be harmed, but it is also possible for him greatly to facilitate the growth of marrows through devoting himself to the study of their nature, needs and preferences and assisting these wherever possible. Nobody can escape self-consciousness, but the child whose parents focus open-mindedly and with interest on what he or she does rather than on what he or she is stands a better chance than most of being able to function in the world as a subject relatively free of the threat of paralysing anxiety.

In many of the institutions we have established for the longer-term care of social casualties – for example, children or people regarded as handicapped in some sense – the care we in fact offer is almost always of the objectifying rather than 'subjectifying' kind. Usually, certainly, there is no lack of the kind of concern and good will which most of us would probably hope to receive in these circumstances, but what *is* often lacking is any recognition of the subjective needs of people whose only real hope of salvation is (like all of us) to be able to stand in an *active* relation to the world in a way which lends *meaning* to their existence. Children in care, for example, may (at least, that is, while they remain in care) in fact be deluged with the kind of material advantages which the average kind-hearted citizen might expect them most to lack and appreciate, and are likely to be surrounded by concerned and dedicated professional staff who take every opportunity to show warmth toward and take an interest in the 'relationships' of their charges. Well meaning local charities collect money for colour televisions and video recorders for the children while social workers attempt to puzzle out and identify the traumata which have marked their experience so that this can be 'talked through' or otherwise taken account of to their benefit. Our collective need towards such children is often an almost desperate one to make up to them for the appalling blows to their objective existence we know them to have suffered, and one can scarcely take exception to the self-denying dedication with which this need is often expressed. What tends not to happen, however, is any real attempt to take seriously the lessons a child may have learned from its experience (however 'deprived' we see this as having been) and to facilitate the possibilities for it to act on its knowledge. We attempt (and inevitably fail) to repair objects rather than help the development of subjects; in trying to 'normalize' those who arouse our compassion we inadvertently deny them the significance of their own experience, and in trying to replace their bitter knowledge of a cruel world with belief in the myths we would prefer to be true, we do them, perhaps, the greatest violence of all.

To heap approval, confirmation and love-as-object upon people, to provide them unstintedly with what so many of us think we want – i.e., to be 'loved for ourselves alone' – may in fact be to do them no great favour since it does nothing very directly to facilitate their development as subjective agents, and leaves them as well vulnerable to annihilation should the source of such love be for any reason withdrawn. To love somebody conditionally as an object is cruel, and to love somebody unconditionally as an object results in empty futility. The individual can only function smoothly when he or she is able to escape from the crippling glare of self-conscious evaluation to make his or her active contribution to the evolution of our world.

There *are* no ways that we *ought* to be other than those which we determine for ourselves. The abandonment of our myths, even though it may free us of the anxiety which arises from self-deception, will not bring us peace of mind, but it may enable us to engage with a real world which we have allowed to get dangerously out of hand.

# Index

Printed in the United States
by Baker & Taylor Publisher Services